WORKING WITH GROUPS IN THE WORKPLACE

BRIDGING THE GENDER GAP

LOUISE YOLTON EBERHARDT

WORKING WITH GROUPS IN THE
WORKPLACE

BRIDGING THE
GENDER
GAP

LOUISE YOLTON EBERHARDT

WHOLE PERSON ASSOCIATES
Duluth, Minnesota

Library of Congress Cataloging in Publication data 94-61706
ISBN 1-57025-023-5

REPRODUCTION POLICY

Printed in the United States of America

10   9   8   7   6   5   4   3   2   1

WHOLE PERSON ASSOCIATES
210 West Michigan
Duluth MN 55802-1908
800-247-6789

To Christopher and David L. and all the women and men struggling to make their lives and our world more humane.

CONTENTS

RESOURCES

INTRODUCTION

We absorb what society considers appropriate behavior through the natural process of socialization, accepting and internalizing cultural ideals without questioning them. These societal "norms" become part of our unconscious gender role belief system—attitudes, attributes, and behaviors we consider appropriate for women and men. We connect masculinity with characteristics such as rationality, aggressiveness, competitiveness, and technical mastery—norms considered desirable in our society and against which it measures both genders. On the other hand, we associate femininity with empathy, nurturing, and receptivity—characteristics on which our society has placed less value.

Negative cultural stereotypes of women—including the idea that women do not need to and should not work outside the home and are less able workers—create problems between men and women, such as discriminatory behavior in the workplace. Fortunately, our culture has begun to acknowledge and discuss how gender socialization has impacted women and men. As a result, many people now attempt to modify gender role prescripts in order to avoid the strains—feelings of inadequacy when they do not fit into their prescribed roles and other problems when they do—built into traditional cultural roles. That modification involves changing how women and men feel, think, and behave.

Awareness is the key to successfully making such complex changes. Groups focusing on gender role issues help participants become aware of the cultural expectations that shape male and female gender role prescripts as well as their corresponding effects on attitudes and behavior. For example, participants learn how society encourages women to repress their need for achievement and men to inhibit their need to express emotions. By providing participants with new information, insights, and models, the group process enables participants to change their perception of society's gender roles and begin to change the behavior shaped by those prescripts.

The exercises in both sections invite participants to "unlearn" the oppression of traditional gender roles, to learn to communicate effectively, to understand equally valid but different points of view, and to discover new ways of relating to one another as partners, friends, and colleagues, as well as begin a new journey toward self-growth.

For information about experiential learning, turn to **How to Use This Book Most Effectively**, which begins on page 159.

Gender
Awareness

GENDER AWARENESS

OVERVIEW

An ideal gender awareness group provides men and women with an opportunity to relate to one another more openly and honestly than our society usually encourages. Through an open communication process, participants can examine the way traditional gender roles have influenced them and continue to affect their lives. They can make discoveries about who they would like to be without culturally-imposed expectations and restrictions.

Participants in gender awareness groups may carry different agendas. Women often seek equal opportunities in education and work. If they have already learned to be more assertive in their interpersonal and sexual relationships with men, they may not feel dependent on men for a definition of themselves. Men, on the other hand, may not know what they want from the group. Some, confused about changing gender roles, may feel somewhat defensive and apprehensive, fearful of attack and nonsupport. Others attend to change themselves—to examine the limitations of their roles and become more open. Some may also want to explore the alienation they feel from women, other men, or even themselves.

Men and women attending as couples may also have varying objectives. A woman may hope to initiate changes in her partner, to seek reinforcement of her feelings, or to grow and change herself (for example, to become more assertive with men). Men may also want self growth, but sometimes resist participating because ambiguity in their present relationship leaves its future unclear—they are reluctant to invest themselves in a failing venture. Because of these varying objectives, clarifying the group's purpose and emphasizing that no time will be given to working on a couple's specific relationship becomes very important. Remind couples that although relationship enrichment could certainly be a by-product of the group, it is not the focus.

GOALS

Major goals of the gender awareness exercises are:

- to examine our society's gender stereotypes and attitudes as a way to heighten awareness of feelings, attitudes, and behaviors.

- to examine the expected behavior of men and women, including ourselves, within those stereotyped roles.

- to discover the impact gender prescripts have had on our career choices, our relationships, and our personal development.

- to form a shared consciousness in which each gender perceives the other more clearly.

- to become more aware of ourselves as people.

- to understand the power dynamics of gender role development and relationships.

- to explore and understand our feelings and behaviors in a mixed-gender group and in a same-gender group.

- to humanize our roles, relationships, and personal lives.

The group may also work on such areas as dependence and independence, anger and caring, and distance and intimacy between women and men.

ASSUMPTIONS

Meeting the goals of a successful gender awareness group relies on the following underlying assumptions:

1. Gender roles are changing in our society today, creating confusion and questions.

2. Gender role expectations develop in a societal context, affecting how we live.

3. Once we examine our culturally-determined assumptions and injunctions, we will have more choices in how we live and who we are.

4. Masculinity—especially that of white, middle-class, heterosexual men—has been the norm against which both genders have been measured. This has led to femininity being seen as a "problem" and women being seen as less healthy human beings. Men of color, working class men, and gay men have also been measured against this norm and have often been found lacking.

5. Our personal and societal images of male and female identity greatly influence our expectations of and our relationships with men and women.

6. Our cultural definitions of femininity and masculinity are based on power dynamics and relationships.

7. From earliest childhood men and women have been socialized so differently they have great difficulty understanding each other, communicating openly and honestly with each other, and being intimate.

©1995 Whole Person Press 210 W Michigan Duluth MN 55802   (800) 247-6789

8. There are few, if any, inherent female or male behavioral characteristics, only human qualities which everyone shares to some degree or another.

9. Each of us is different regarding our exploration of our gender identity and how we view and relate to others. Our concerns about gender issues change over time and are also influenced by our skin color, ethnic group, class, sexual orientation, region, and nationality.

10. As we increase awareness of our individual problems, we discover common problems stemming from our cultural conditioning.

11. No real structural changes in gender roles and institutions can occur among women alone—the focus must expand to consider the many ways men's gender roles affect them, the costs and privileges of gender roles, and the roles of humans as inhabitants of the earth.

WORKSHOP STRUCTURE

A gender role awareness group works best when planned for a weekend or for weekly meetings. About eight to ten sessions with groups ranging in size from ten to twenty participants work best. An equal number of male and female members maximizes effectiveness; however, a slight difference in the number of men to women is manageable.

The exercises in this section can also be used as part of training workshops for diversity, couples' therapy or marriage enrichment, college classes, or youth seminars.

1 THE COCKTAIL PARTY

A new twist on the old-fashioned social mixer, this introductory exercise helps participants identify male and female social interaction patterns.

GOALS

To identify male and female behavior common in mixed-gender groups.

To examine our individual gender role patterns.

GROUP SIZE

Unlimited; most effective if gender groups can be divided equally.

TIME

$1^1/_2$ hours.

MATERIALS

Wine, juice, or soda; snacks; music cassettes or CDs and appropriate playback equipment; pencils; magic markers; masking tape; easels and easel paper; **Mixer Reflection Questions** worksheet.

PROCESS

☞ *This exercise should be the first activity in a workshop.*

Activity 1: Mixer

1. Have wine (if appropriate), soda, or juice available and music playing as participants enter. Let events occur naturally until all arrive or approximately 15 minutes after the official starting time has elapsed. Facilitators should interact and observe.

2. Introduce the activity with the following information:

   • We began this session from the time you walked in the door.

   • You probably experienced several different feelings during that time as you began to encounter others or chose to be alone.

   • We are now going to spend some time alone considering those feelings and examining what happened.

3. Distribute the worksheet and allow participants 10 minutes to fill it out.

©1995 Whole Person Press 210 W Michigan Duluth MN 55802   (800) 247-6789

4. Form same-gender triads and ask participants to discuss their answers to the worksheet questions.

5. After 20 minutes, reconvene the entire group, have the female participants and facilitators form a circle in the center of the room, and provide the following instructions:

   ➤ The women will have 20 minutes to share their personal feelings about what happened in the mixer activity.

   ➤ The men should listen silently.

   ☞ *Facilitators need to help the group focus on their gender behavior and the gender behavior of the other group.*

6. After 15 minutes, call time and reverse the process, placing the men in the inner circle.

7. Ask participants for their observations and insights concerning male and female behavior in a mixed group.

Activity 2: Examining My Behavior

1. Divide participants into same-gender groups and move them to different parts of the room.

2. Ask each group to consider how they interact in a mixed-gender group and identify the behaviors they would like to continue or change.

3. Reconvene the entire group and invite each group to share highlights from their discussions.

VARIATION

■ If the group enjoys a diversity of members from other groups (racial, age, sexual orientation, etc.), discuss how dynamics of those groups also effected their interactions.

©1995 Whole Person Press 210 W Michigan Duluth MN 55802   (800) 247-6789

MIXER REFLECTION QUESTIONS

1. How did you feel about yourself as you walked through the door?

2. What did you hope would happen during the first few minutes?

3. What did you do or not do to help it happen? Is this normally how you would behave in a mixed-gender group? Explain.

4. As a result of what did happen, how do you now feel about yourself (powerful, weak, angry, satisfied, dissatisfied, etc.)?

5. How did you feel about the women's behavior? About the men's?

6. What patterns, if any, did you notice in the behavior of the women? the men?

7. How did you feel about what was happening in the group during this time? What did you do with those feelings?

©1995 Whole Person Press 210 W Michigan Duluth MN 55802   (800) 247-6789

2 SELF-FULFILLMENT

After taking a "self-fulfillment" inventory, participants introduce themselves to the group by sharing their self-perceptions and which gender areas they would like to explore during the workshop.

GOALS

To increase awareness of our individual self-fulfillment.

To identify gender growth areas participants wish to explore.

To allow participants an opportunity to learn more about one another.

GROUP SIZE

10–20 participants.

TIME

1 hour.

MATERIALS

Easels and easel paper; magic markers; masking tape; **Self-Fulfillment Inventory** worksheets; **Self-Fulfillment Inventory Reflection Questions** worksheet.

PROCESS

Activity 1: Self Reflection

1. Introduce the exercise by sharing the following information:
   - This exercise will help you identify your level of self-fulfillment.
   - We will also identify gender issues you may wish to explore during future sessions.
   - You will take an inventory to assess your level of personal fulfillment.
   - You will also examine areas in which men and women are thought to differ greatly.

2. Distribute the **Self-Fulfillment Inventory** worksheets and provide the following instructions:

©1995 Whole Person Press 210 W Michigan Duluth MN 55802   (800) 247-6789

> ➤ In order to fully benefit from the exercise, your answers must be completely honest.

> ➤ There are no right or wrong answers.

> ➤ Afterwards we will discuss our inventories, but you only have to talk about answers you feel comfortable sharing.

3. When they have completed the **Self-Fulfillment Inventory** worksheets, distribute the **Self-Fulfillment Inventory Reflection Questions** worksheet and allow participants 5 minutes to complete it using their replies to the first worksheet as a basis for their answers.

Activity 2: Sharing

1. Have participants find a same-gender partner and discuss the **Self-Fulfillment Inventory** worksheet, sharing whatever they want about their responses and any insights they gained filling it out.

2. After 10 minutes, have participants form mixed-gender pairs and discuss their responses to and insights gained from the questions on the **Self-Fulfillment Inventory Reflection Questions** worksheet.

3. Reconvene the entire group and have participants introduce themselves by sharing the following:

   • An area of strength, of strong personal satisfaction

   • An area for growth, of little personal satisfaction

   • One or two gender issues or areas he or she would like to explore in future sessions

4. Ask participants for any gender generalizations or patterns they may have observed during *Step 3*.

5. Discuss which gender issues they mentioned in *Step 3* can and will be covered during the group sessions.

VARIATIONS

■ In *Step 4* of Activity 2, discuss stereotypes of typical male and female problems and whether they are true for the group.

SELF-FULFILLMENT INVENTORY

Instructions: Circle the number that represents your level of satisfaction. 1 = totally disagree; 10 = totally agree.

1. Overall, I am satisfied with myself as a man or woman.

   1 2 3 4 5 6 7 8 9 10

2. I have close relationships with people of my own gender.

   1 2 3 4 5 6 7 8 9 10

3. I have close relationships with people of the other gender.

   1 2 3 4 5 6 7 8 9 10

4. I have significant intimate relationship(s).

   1 2 3 4 5 6 7 8 9 10

5. I have close relationships with children.

   1 2 3 4 5 6 7 8 9 10

6. I know what I want:

   a. from women   1 2 3 4 5 6 7 8 9 10

   b. from men   1 2 3 4 5 6 7 8 9 10

7. I ask for what I want:

   a. from women   1 2 3 4 5 6 7 8 9 10

   b. from men   1 2 3 4 5 6 7 8 9 10

8. I am aware of what I am feeling.

   1 2 3 4 5 6 7 8 9 10

9. I can directly and honestly express my feelings, including anger, tenderness, sorrow, fear, and joy, appropriately:

   a. to women   1 2 3 4 5 6 7 8 9 10

   b. to men   1 2 3 4 5 6 7 8 9 10

10. I feel satisfied with the current condition and appearance of my body.

    1 2 3 4 5 6 7 8 9 10

SELF-FULFILLMENT INVENTORY, continued

11. I take care of my body.

        1 2 3 4 5 6 7 8 9 10

12. I can fully experience my sexuality.

        1 2 3 4 5 6 7 8 9 10

13. I am pleased with the quality of my inner life.

        1 2 3 4 5 6 7 8 9 10

14. I can comfortably give affection:

    a. to women   1 2 3 4 5 6 7 8 9 10

    b. to men   1 2 3 4 5 6 7 8 9 10

15. I can comfortably receive affection:

    a. from women   1 2 3 4 5 6 7 8 9 10

    b. from men   1 2 3 4 5 6 7 8 9 10

16. I make a contribution to my community and the world.

        1 2 3 4 5 6 7 8 9 10

17. I am fulfilled in my chosen work.

        1 2 3 4 5 6 7 8 9 10

18. I am pleased with my achievements in my chosen field.

        1 2 3 4 5 6 7 8 9 10

19. I enjoy my life.

        1 2 3 4 5 6 7 8 9 10

20. I am free of stereotypes or role expectations:

    a. of women   1 2 3 4 5 6 7 8 9 10

    b. of men   1 2 3 4 5 6 7 8 9 10

    c. of myself   1 2 3 4 5 6 7 8 9 10

21. I have integrity, a clear set of values which I live by.

        1 2 3 4 5 6 7 8 9 10

©1995 Whole Person Press 210 W Michigan Duluth MN 55802   (800) 247-6789

SELF-FULFILLMENT INVENTORY
REFLECTION QUESTIONS

1. In which areas of life are you very fulfilled? Are these typical strengths for your gender?

2. In which areas of life are you not very fulfilled—areas for growth? Are these typical growth areas for your gender?

3. What changes would you like to see in your relationships with men? with women?

4. What gender issues do you want to explore?

3 POLARITIES

In this active introductory exercise, participants find themselves in several different groups, exploring assumptions they make about their own group and others.

GOALS

To identify the assumptions we make about gender groups.

To break the ice in a group that will be discussing diversity issues.

GROUP SIZE

Unlimited.

TIME

$1^1/_2$ hours.

MATERIALS

Easel and easel paper; magic markers; masking tape.

PROCESS

1. Briefly introduce the exercise with the following chalktalk points:

   • We are going to spend some time examining our feelings and the assumptions we make about gender groups.

   • This exercise will help us get acquainted and will serve as a warm up activity to help us get into the spirit of the workshop.

   • We'll be moving around the room, meeting each other in various ways and participating in several different groups.

   • In each group you will discuss how it feels to be a member of a group, and your assumptions about members of other groups.

   • The first groups will be separated by gender.

2. Ask all the women to go to the front of the room and all the men to go to the back.

   ☞ *Have facilitators stand with groups appropriate to their gender.*

3. Have facilitators present the task: the women are to discuss how it feels to be in the female group and the men how it feels to be in the male group.

☞ *Record their feelings on an easel chart.*

4. After 10 minutes, ask each group to discuss their assumptions about the other group's feelings.

   ☞ *Record these assumptions on an easel chart.*

5. Reconvene the entire group and ask each gender group to read the lists generated in *Step 3*.

   ☞ *Allow only questions of clarification from the other group.*

6. Ask each gender group to read the lists generated in *Step 4*.

7. Repeat *Steps 2–6* using two or three other significant polarities present in the group.

   ☞ *Suggested polarities include age (young, middle age, senior citizens), race (people of color and white people), marital status (married and single).*

8. After exploring two or more polarities, invite participants to share any insights they may have gained during the activity.

9. Summarize the central themes and impressions mentioned by participants in *Step 8*.

VARIATIONS

■ To help participants examine gender differences, use personal characteristics such as passive/aggressive, rational/emotional, leader/follower, feminine/masculine, gentle/forceful instead of the suggested polarities. Ask them to go to the group with which they identify most.

■ If you want to focus more specifically on gender, consider having them identify how it feels to be a male or a female member of the other polarity groups. For example, if race is used, discuss how it feels to be a woman of color or a man of color, a white woman or a white man.

©1995 Whole Person Press 210 W Michigan Duluth MN 55802   (800) 247-6789

4 WHO AM I?

Participants pair up with someone of the opposite gender to share their self-perceptions—a quick theme expander that gets everyone involved and helps them focus on gender roles.

GOALS

To become more aware of how participants see themselves.

To provide an opportunity for participants to introduce themselves.

To learn more about each other and oneself.

GROUP SIZE

Unlimited; most effective if gender groups can be divided equally.

TIME

45 minutes.

MATERIALS

Easel and easel paper; magic markers; masking tape; **"Who I Am?"** **Reflection Questions** worksheet.

PROCESS

Activity 1: I Am

1. Have participants move around the room and find a partner of the other gender, then provide the following instructions:

    ➤ Choose who will go first.

    ➤ That person will tell the other person who he or she is by completing sentences beginning with "I am . . . "

    ➤ Complete as many "I am" sentences as you can in one minute.

    ➤ The other person just listens—do not respond to your partner's statements.

    ➤ After 1 minute I will call time and ask you to switch roles.

    ➤ The first partner has 1 minute. Begin.

2. After 1 minute, stop the first partner and ask the pairs to switch roles.

3. At the end of 1 minute, stop the second partner and have each participant find a new partner of the other gender. Instruct them to repeat *Step 1* without duplicating anything they said to their first partner.

4. Repeat *Step 2*.

Activity 2: Reflection

1. Form mixed-gender groups of 4 and distribute the worksheets, asking participants to spend 25 minutes discussing the questions.

   ☞ *Circulate from group to group, listening and acting as a consultant where needed.*

2. When most groups have finished, reconvene the entire group and invite participants to share what they learned during the discussion.

VARIATION

■ Repeat Activity 1, having them form pairs with someone of the same gender. Reconvene the group and ask them to discuss the difference between what they shared with members of the other gender and members of their own gender.

"WHO AM I?" REFLECTION QUESTIONS

1. What were your feelings during the activity?

2. Was there a change in what you shared? For example, did you start with "safe" revelations about yourself and later move to more vulnerable areas?

3. Consider the descriptions of yourself you started with and the ones you ended with. Which are the closest to how you see yourself? Which are the closest to the cultural stereotypes of your gender?

4. Is there ever a difference between who you feel you are and how you project yourself to others? For example, "I am sometimes weak; I pretend that I am always strong."

5. What did you learn about the other gender?

5 BUILDING TRUST

In this open, sharing exercise, participants reveal information about themselves, helping to build trust and openness between genders in the group.

GOALS

To build trust and openness between genders.

To help participants become more comfortable disclosing their views of gender topics.

GROUP SIZE

Unlimited (but requires a facilitator for every group of 6–8 participants).

TIME

$1\frac{1}{2}$ hours.

MATERIALS

None.

PROCESS

Activity 1: Self-Disclosure

1. Announce that the exercise will encourage disclosure of participants views regarding gender issues.

2. Form mixed-gender groups of 6–8 participants, assign a facilitator to each group, and move each group to a separate room or space.

3. Have each small group facilitator introduce the activity by explaining the exercise's process:

   • In order to get better acquainted and begin to examine some of our attitudes toward men and women, I am going to give each of you a number of open-ended sentences to complete.

   • We will go around the circle, with each person answering in turn.

4. Read the first question and go around the group, allowing each participant an opportunity to answer it, including yourself. Continue to present as many questions as you wish and time allows.

☞ *Choose the open-ended sentences you will use ahead of time.*
Stop if you feel the group is getting tired or too saturated with
data. Ten or twelve questions is usually the limit.

Activity 2: Reflection

1. When everyone has had a chance to complete each sentence, ask the
   group to discuss the experience using the following questions:

   ✔ How do you feel right now?

   ✔ Do you feel different than when we started? If so, why?

   ✔ When were you most open and honest?

   ✔ When did you hold back?

   ✔ Which questions were comfortable to answer? Which were uncomfortable? Explain.

   ✔ What have you learned about men and women?

2. Reconvene the entire group and have participants share what they
   learned during the exercise.

VARIATIONS

■ Instead of using those suggested, make up your own questions with
topics more appropriate to your particular group.

■ If the group has no more than 15 members, do not divide them into
smaller groups. This will help build even more trust within the group.

Building Trust Open-Ended Questions

• If I could be anyone besides myself, I would be . . .

• If I could take a trip to anywhere right now, I would go to . . . and
take . . . with me.

• If I could be a historical character, I would choose to be . . .

• If I were a character in a novel or play, I would be . . .

• The features of my personality I am most proud of include . . .

• The features of my personality I am least proud of include . . .

• The features of my appearance I consider the most attractive to
members of the other gender include . . .

- The features of my appearance I consider least attractive to members of the other gender include . . .

- Roles or games I sometimes find myself playing with members of the other gender include . . .

- Characteristics or traits I want most in a friend of the same gender include . . .

- When I first meet a member of the other gender, I usually . . .

- What I like about how members of the other gender interact with me is . . .

- What I don't like about how members of the other gender interact with me is . . .

- If I could have an ideal relationship with someone, it would include . . .

- What I want to change about my sex life is . . .

©1995 Whole Person Press 210 W Michigan Duluth MN 55802   (800) 247-6789

6 "TYPICAL" BEHAVIOR

Participants explore their gender expectations and identify the costs and benefits of changing stereotypical role expectations of themselves and others.

GOALS

To examine stereotypical gender roles.

To explore feelings when women and men engage in atypical gender role behavior.

To identify expectations we have of the other gender and the costs and benefits that may accompany changing those expectations.

GROUP SIZE

20 participants (works with other group sizes, but not as well).

TIME

1 hour.

MATERIALS

None.

PROCESS

Activity 1: Gender Role Expectations of Self

1. Explain that this exercise helps participants explore gender role behavior.

2. Ask each participant to share something they do that our society considers stereotypical or expected behavior for their gender (for example, ironing for women, yard work for men).

3. Initiate a discussion using the following question:

   ✔ How comfortable are you while performing tasks expected of you simply because you are either a man or a woman?

4. Ask each participant to share something they do that our society considers atypical or not expected behavior for their gender (for example, laundry for men, fixing a car for women).

5. Create a discussion using the following questions:

✔ What is your degree of comfort performing tasks not expected of you simply because you are either a woman or a man?

✔ What type of responses do you receive from others when you engage in behaviors expected of your gender?

✔ What type of responses do you receive from others when you engage in behaviors not expected of your gender?

✔ Would you like to do more things considered atypical of your gender, but do you hold back because of possible negative reactions or perceptions from others? If yes, what do you hold back from doing?

✔ What did you notice or learn during this activity?

Activity 2: Expectations of the Other Gender

1. Divide participants into same-gender groups and place them in separate meeting spaces.

2. Ask each group to discuss the following questions:

☞ *Facilitators may want to record their answers on an easel.*

✔ What stereotypical behavior do you expect from the other gender?

✔ How do you feel about these expectations?

✔ Which of your other-gender expectations would you like to change?

✔ How would you benefit if you changed these expectations?

✔ What would you lose if you changed these expectations?

3. Reconvene the entire group and encourage participants to share what they learned during the activity.

VARIATIONS

■ As an addition to Activity 2, have participants share the role expectations they have of their own gender and how they feel when someone steps out of that role.

■ Conclude by having participants pair with someone of their own gender and ask them to share an insight they might not normally share with someone of that gender. Then have them meet with a member of the other gender to share an insight they might not normally share with that gender.

7 GENDER ROLE TIME LINE

In this creative exercise, participants sketch significant sex role messages they have received throughout their life in order to better understand how those ideas shape their gender perceptions.

GOALS

To identify significant gender messages women and men receive throughout their lives.

To examine the differences between and similarities among gender messages received during various time periods.

To be creative and have some fun.

GROUP SIZE

10–30 participants.

TIME

2 hours.

MATERIALS

Butcher paper; magic markers (30–40 of many different colors); masking tape.

PROCESS

☞ *Before beginning this session, cover two walls with newsprint, one labelled "Women's Messages" and the other "Men's Messages." Draw a time line and identify times/ages on each gender's paper that fit the age of your participants (for example, the times/ages for a group with the widest variety of ages would include infant to preschool, elementary school, junior high school, high school, college or young adulthood, middle age, late adult years.)*

1. Introduce the exercise by making the following points:

   • Today we will explore the messages we have received about ourselves as girls, boys, men, and women.

   • We want to focus on those gender messages that helped develop and continue to reinforce our gender identities.

©1995 Whole Person Press 210 W Michigan Duluth MN 55802   (800) 247-6789

- Think about the significant gender role messages you received at various stages of your life.

- For instance, at some point when you were young you probably heard "big boys don't cry" or "nice girls don't kiss on the first date."

- In a minute I will ask you to draw some of those messages on the paper you see on the wall. Have fun drawing and don't worry about your artistic talent.

  ☞ *You may get some groans and comments: "I can't draw." Be encouraging and participants will usually get involved. You can also allow them to use some key words if you wish.*

2. Point out the time lines for the male and female messages and provide the following instructions:

➤ Take some markers and move to your gender's side of the room.

➤ Depict messages you received by drawing vignettes or symbols by the various ages of your life.

➤ You may interact with the drawings of others, but should not talk while drawing.

➤ You have 20 minutes. Begin.

3. After 20 minutes (or when most have stopped drawing) have participants mill about the room to examine the images drawn by both groups.

4. Reconvene the entire group and ask the women's group to talk about the messages depicted in their pictures as the men listen.

5. When the women have finished sharing, invite the men to ask questions.

6. Repeat *Steps 4* and *5* with the men's group explaining their drawings.

7. Discuss what they learned about gender role identity and how gender messages affected their lives and relationships, and how they interact with members of their own and the other gender.

VARIATIONS

■ Conduct *Steps 4–6* by alternating gender groups along the time line (i.e., first the women discuss junior high messages, followed by the men; next, both groups discuss senior high, etc.).

■ Exercise 24, Themes and Myths, makes an excellent follow-up exercise to this one.

8 GENDER COMMANDMENTS

In this reflective exercise, participants examine the major "command-ments" they have received about being male or female.

GOALS

To identify the major gender prescripts we have received and continue to receive.

To understand how these prescripts influence our thinking and behavior.

GROUP SIZE

10–30 participants.

TIME

2 hours.

MATERIALS

Easels and easel paper; magic markers; masking tape; **Ten Gender Commandments for Men** worksheet; **Ten Gender Commandments for Women** worksheet.

PROCESS

☞ *This activity works best after Exercises 7 or 21, (the socialization messages exercises) either of which will help participants begin to think about major gender-socialization themes.*

1. Begin the exercise by telling the participants that they will identify and examine gender messages they received through socialization.

2. Divide participants into same-gender groups and have them move to separate spaces or rooms.

3. Distribute copies of the **Ten Gender Commandments for Men** worksheets to the men's group and the **Ten Gender Commandments for Women** worksheets to the women's group while providing the following instructions:

   ➤ Think about all the messages you have received about your gender role and try to condense them into ten major "commandments."

   ➤ Write them down on your worksheet.

☞ *They may need an example to help get started. Examples for men might include: "Thou shalt dominate and control people, events, and objects;" "Thou shalt not be responsible for housework;" "Thou shalt not be vulnerable, but respect the logical." Examples for women might include: "Thou shalt stay young and attractive;" "Thou shalt nurture and give to others before thyself;" "Thou shalt protect men's egos;" "Thou shalt not acknowledge unpleasant feelings, especially anger."*

4. After about 5 minutes, ask participants to share what they wrote with the other members of their group, develop a group list of ten commandments, and record them on an easel.

5. Once the lists are complete, have the groups discuss how these commandments have influenced their thinking and behavior.

6. Reconvene the entire group and ask each gender group to share their list of commandments.

7. Form mixed-gender groups of 6 participants to discuss the commandments using the following questions:

   ☞ *Post the questions on a easel so all can see.*

   ✔ How have these commandments caused problems for you?

   ✔ How do these commandments affect your relationships with members of the other gender?

   ✔ How do these commandments affect your relationships with members of your own gender group?

8. After about 20 minutes, ask the groups to develop some healthier commandments for women and men and record them on an easel.

   ☞ *If their lists are longer than 10 items, have them eliminate the least important ones or combine items.*

9. Reconvene the entire group and ask the groups to report their lists.

10. Note common themes and differences.

TEN GENDER COMMANDMENTS FOR MEN

Instructions: Write down 10 or more "commandments" that you have received or continue to receive about what you, as a man, should and should not do.

1.

2.

3.

4.

5.

6.

7.

8.

9.

10.

TEN GENDER COMMANDMENTS FOR WOMEN

Instructions: Write down 10 or more "commandments" that you have received or continue to receive about what you, as a woman, should and should not do.

1.

2.

3.

4.

5.

6.

7.

8.

9.

10.

9 REVERSE GENDER FANTASY

In this guided fantasy exercise, participants imagine what it would be like to become the other gender.

GOALS

To think about, explore, and become more aware of what it would be like to be the other gender.

GROUP SIZE

Unlimited (but requires a facilitator for every group of 7 participants).

TIME

2 hours.

MATERIALS

None.

PROCESS

Activity 1: Ice Breaker

1. Ask the following question as an ice breaker:

   ✔ If you were going to be reincarnated and were considering only how much pleasure you would experience in your next lifetime, would you choose to return as a man or a woman?

2. Ask those that would return as a woman to raise their hands.

3. Ask those that would return as a man to raise their hands.

4. Ask the group members who chose to return as women to share the reasons for their choice.

5. Ask the group members who chose to return as men to share the reasons for their choice.

6. Lead a brief discussion regarding what participants noticed about their choices.

©1995 Whole Person Press 210 W Michigan Duluth MN 55802   (800) 247-6789

Activity 2: Reverse Fantasy

1. Instruct participants to find a comfortable position in the room—
either lying down or sitting comfortably with feet on the floor—and
then tell them:

   • Now you will all have an opportunity to explore what it would be
   like to become the other gender.

   • Close your eyes and try to imagine and experience what I read to you.

2. Slowly read the **Reverse Guided Fantasy** script.

   ☞ *Be sure to read slowly and pause at the ellipses (. . .) to allow
   participants to imagine what you describe.*

3. When you have finished and participants have returned their attention
to the group, form mixed-gender groups of 6 or 7 participants and
have them use the following questions to share their observations and
insights:

   ✔ Were you able to "become" the other gender? If it was difficult for
   you, what made it difficult?

   ☞ *Men often have a difficult time imagining themselves female.
   Do not judge this, but encourage them to share what made it
   difficult. Women often experience tremendous feelings of
   power and safety imagining themselves male and it is important for them to share these feelings as well.*

   ✔ What issues did this activity bring up for you?

   ✔ What did you feel as someone of the other gender?

   ✔ What new insights do you have about the other gender? about your
   own gender?

VARIATIONS

   ■ Develop a more specific fantasy about being the other gender, revers-
   ing the roles of men and women. For example, women run the
   country, we have a woman president, only 2 male senators, and most
   company CEO's are women; men do most of the housework and act as
   the primary nurturers.

Reverse Gender Fantasy Script

*Close your eyes and release your tension. . . . Adjust your body so you are
comfortable. . . . Focus on your breathing and continue to let go as I speak. . . .*

In a moment you will have an opportunity to alter the way you experience yourself and parts of your world. But for the next minute just take some deep breaths and let them out gently. . . .

Now I'd like you to imagine that your gender has been reversed. If you are a man, you are now a woman; if you are a woman, you are now a man. . . .

Notice the changes in your physical self. Your body is different now. . . . Become very aware of this new body, especially those parts that have changed. . . .

How does your new body feel? . . . weaker? stronger? softer? more forceful? . . . What kinds of things can you do in this new body? . . . What won't you be able to do in this new body? . . .

In what ways will your life be different now? . . . at work? . . . in your personal life? . . . How will you be viewed by others? . . . by society as a whole? . . . What new roles do you have in society? . . . How will that impact you? . . .

What can or will you do differently now that your gender has changed? What new fears, concerns, and hopes do you have? . . .

How do you feel about all these changes? . . . Continue to explore what it would be like to experience being the other gender. . . .

Now return to your own body and become yourself again. . . . Compare how it feels to be your own gender to the experience of being the other gender. . . . What are you aware of? . . . What is positive about being your gender? . . . What is negative? . . .

Take a minute or two and slowly come back to the room; open your eyes when you are ready.

©1995 Whole Person Press 210 W Michigan Duluth MN 55802   (800) 247-6789

10 ANDROGYNY

Participants identify their level of androgyny and what areas or skills each needs to develop further in order to become a more balanced, whole person.

GOALS

To understand the concept and value of androgyny.

To examine whether participants define themselves as masculine, feminine, or androgynous.

To identify which areas men and women need to work on in order to become more balanced.

GROUP SIZE

10–30 participants.

TIME

2 hours.

MATERIALS

Easels and easel paper; magic markers; masking tape; **Personal Strengths** worksheet; **The Androgynous Person** worksheet.

PROCESS

Activity 1: Personal Strengths

☞ *Do not share the title of the exercise or its goals at this point.*

1. Distribute the **Personal Strengths** worksheet with the following instructions:

    ➤ This inventory contains a list of traits or characteristics most people see as individual strengths.

    ➤ Take a few minutes to read each column and check the box next to your strengths, those traits others and you would consider your strong points.

2. When all have finished, provide the following information about the inventory:

- This inventory contains what most people traditionally consider both strong male and strong female traits.

- Starting at the top of the list, the first trait is feminine; the second is masculine. Feminine and masculine traits alternate through the rest of the list.

3. Have participants go through the list again, marking an "F" next to the boxes beside the feminine traits and an "M" next to the boxes beside the masculine traits.

4. When they have finished, distribute the **The Androgynous Person** worksheets and have participants write the feminine and masculine characteristics they checked as their personal strengths under the appropriate heading.

Activity 2: Androgyny Chalktalk

1. Introduce the concept of androgyny with the following chalktalk:

- Both historically and cross-culturally, masculinity and femininity seem to represent two complementary lists of positive traits and behaviors.

- As adults, we have to be able to take care of ourselves and get things done, which requires the ability to be assertive, independent, and self-reliant—characteristics men are suppose to have.

- Traditionally, women were not supposed to have these characteristics.

- An adult also needs to be able to relate and communicate effectively with others; be sensitive to others' needs; show warmth, caring, and affection; and be open to emotional support from others—characteristics women are supposed to have.

- Traditionally, men were not supposed to have any of these characteristics.

- Many think an androgynous person is a healthy adult who exhibits neither strong feminine nor strong masculine behavior; rather she or he is able to exhibit whatever trait is appropriate to a given situation and has the best of both feminine and masculine traits as strengths.

- The word androgyny derives from two Greek words: *andros* and *gyne*, man and woman.

- The androgynous person can be strong and tender, feeling and rational, receptive and independent, etc.

- We can all become more androgynous—whole persons, free to select from a variety of behaviors that suit a variety of situations.

2. Ask participants to look at their **The Androgynous Person** worksheets and see if they have a balance of masculine and feminine traits or if generally they have strengths common to only one gender.

3. Share some interpretations of what their worksheets may mean, based on current gender role research:

   - Women with most of their strengths on the feminine side and men with most of their strengths on the masculine side traditionally fit into their gender's stereotyped role and experience more anxiety, lower self-esteem, and neurosis.

   - Women with extreme femininity often demonstrate dependency and self-denial. They may fear taking initiative or risks. On the other hand, men with high masculinity may exhibit arrogance, tend to exploit others, and may even have violent tendencies.

   - Androgynous persons, those with a list of more balanced feminine and masculine strengths, tend to be creative and flexible, less stressed and anxious, and even more nurturing than women who are highly feminine.

   - It is possible for men to have more of their strengths on the feminine side and vice versa. This is not negative and often indicates high creativity and intellectual development. Professional women often tend to have many strengths traditionally associated with masculinity.

4. Ask participants if they have any questions about androgyny.

   ☞ *If you have a person who did not identify any or only a few strengths on either side, they may have a very low self-concept. You might suggest they are being too hard on themselves and encourage them to take another look at their worksheet, adding some strengths.*

5. Conclude with comments such as:

   - In order to become a whole and healthier person, each of us needs to become more androgynous.

   - Today more and more organizations are looking for androgynous managers and employees.

   - In the next activity, we will examine what each of us needs to develop to become more whole, balanced, androgynous persons.

Activity 3: Becoming More Androgynous

1. Form same-gender groups and ask participants to develop a list of behaviors their gender needs to develop to become more androgynous.

    ☞ *It is helpful to look at the* **Personal Strengths** *as clues as to what is needed. Most men need to concentrate on the following areas:*

    - *Developing the ability to be aware of and express personal feelings*

    - *Increasing interpersonal communication skills such as listening and being open and honest*

    - *Developing closer relationships with other men and becoming less homophobic*

    - *Developing nurturing skills*

    Most women need to work on the following:

    - *Developing assertiveness skills*

    - *Taking risks and overcoming fears*

    - *Developing the ability to focus on the big picture and be more task-oriented*

    - *Developing problem solving and analytical skills*

    - *Exhibiting less self-blame*

    - *Networking with and supporting other women*

2. Reconvene the entire group and have each gender group report their lists using the following process:

    a. Have the women sit in the center and read their group list.

    b. Have each woman share one or two things she needs to develop to become more androgynous.

    c. Repeat *Steps a* and *b* with the men in the center.

3. Encourage participants to share any insights they gained from the activity.

4. Form same-gender groups of 3 and have them discuss how they can support one another in their self-development.

VARIATIONS

■ In *Step 4* of Activity 3, form mixed-gender groups of 4 instead of same-gender groups of 3 so participants can gain a variety of insights.

PERSONAL STRENGTHS

- ❏ Loyal
- ❏ Self-reliant
- ❏ Feminine
- ❏ Defends own beliefs
- ❏ Warm
- ❏ Forceful
- ❏ Expressive
- ❏ Athletic
- ❏ Intuitive
- ❏ Aggressive
- ❏ Tender
- ❏ Analytical
- ❏ Cheerful
- ❏ Rational
- ❏ Affectionate
- ❏ Ambitious
- ❏ Soothes hurt feelings
- ❏ Takes risks, courageous
- ❏ Receptive to others' ideas

- ❏ Decisive
- ❏ Understanding
- ❏ Acts as a leader
- ❏ Gentle
- ❏ Willing to take a stand
- ❏ Sensitive to others' needs
- ❏ Competitive
- ❏ Being oriented
- ❏ Strong personality
- ❏ Aware of own needs
- ❏ Task-oriented
- ❏ Passive
- ❏ Masculine
- ❏ Soft-spoken
- ❏ Individualistic
- ❏ Compassionate
- ❏ Dominant
- ❏ Supportive
- ❏ Take charge attitude

©1995 Whole Person Press 210 W Michigan Duluth MN 55802 (800) 247-6789

THE ANDROGYNOUS PERSON

Masculine Traits	Feminine Traits

11 IDEAL LIFE PARTNER

In this unique exercise, participants write an advertisement for their ideal partner and receive feedback about their preferences.

GOALS

To become more aware of the type of person with whom we want to have an intimate relationship.

To receive feedback from others regarding our ideal life partner.

To gain insight about the important issues involved in partner choice.

GROUP SIZE

15–20 participants; most effective if gender groups can be divided equally.

TIME

2$^1/_2$ hours.

MATERIALS

Easels and easel paper; magic markers (dark colors, one for each participant); masking tape; pens and pencils; **Ideal Life Partner** worksheet.

PROCESS

Activity 1: Ideal Descriptions

1. Introduce the exercise by explaining that it is designed to help them explore partner choices, expectations, and ideal and real relationships.

2. Distribute the **Ideal Life Partner** worksheet and provide the following instructions:

    ➤ Write a "personal" ad describing your ideal life partner—the exact type of person with whom you would like to spend the rest of your life.

    ➤ The worksheet includes some major categories, but feel free to add your own.

    ➤ You have 15 minutes.

3. When all have finished, give each participant a sheet of easel paper, a marker, and the following instructions:

➤ Now write your worksheet description on the easel paper.

➤ When you have finished, post your easel sheets on the wall.

Activity 2: Descriptions Feedback

1. Instruct the group to mill about the room and read each advertisement.

2. When they have finished, tell them to sign their name on the description that best describes who they are or who they would like to be.

3. Spend 5 to 10 minutes using the following questions to discuss how each advertisement affected the group:

   ✔ What aspects of the description caused some to sign their names and others not to?

   ✔ Was the description gender stereotypical, romantic, plastic, wholesome and balanced, unrealistic, etc.?

   ✔ What expectations would you hold for the partner described? What might they expect from the person who wrote the ad?

Activity 3: Partner Choice

1. Form mixed-gender groups of 4–6 participants.

2. Have them discuss what they learned in Activities 1 and 2 by answering the following questions:

   ✔ Overall, what did you learn about your partner choices?

   ✔ Is there any relationship between your ideal and present partner?

   ✔ What is your level of satisfaction in your current relationship(s)?

   ✔ Have your past relationships been based more on romance or on such things as shared values and friendship?

   ✔ What gender issues affect your current (or have affected your past) relationships (i.e., intimacy/distance, power/control, etc.)?

   ✔ Have you made any decisions regarding your choice of partners?

3. Reconvene the entire group and invite participants to share what they have learned.

VARIATIONS

■ For an in-depth examination of relationships, use the Relationship Patterns chart in Exercise 26 of *Working with Women's Groups, Volume 1* (published by Whole Person Associates).

©1995 Whole Person Press 210 W Michigan Duluth MN 55802   (800) 247-6789

IDEAL LIFE PARTNER

I am looking for an ideal life partner with the following . . .

Personality:

Physical characteristics:

Sexuality:

Relationship behaviors (including intimacy/distance and power/control):

General behavior (around other people):

Values and interests:

Other:

12 GENDER MASKS

Participants construct and wear "gender masks" to symbolically explore what it would be like to "take off" the masks they wear to protect themselves.

GOALS

To examine the masks we often present to others.

To experience being more open and vulnerable to others.

To explore the connection between the gender masks we wear and our level of self-esteem.

GROUP SIZE

10–30 participants.

TIME

2 hours.

MATERIALS

Easel and easel paper; paper bags; art supplies; magic markers (30–40 of different colors); masking tape; **Gender Masks I Wear** worksheet; **Common Gender Masks** worksheet.

PROCESS

Activity 1: Ice Breaker

1. Ask each person to answer the following questions:

   ✔ What words or thoughts does the word "intimacy" bring to mind?

   ☞ *Record replies on an easel. If no one else does, mention that intimacy involves taking off our public masks—to be our true selves with one another.*

   ✔ What are your fears about being intimate?

2. Discuss their answers and identify any commonalities, especially between men and women.

Activity 2: Masks

1. Introduce the exercise by outlining the following concepts:

   • During our gender socialization, most of us learn that we should hide or repress some of our thoughts, feelings, and behaviors because they may not be seen as acceptable for our gender to exhibit.

   • Men, for example, may feel grief or sadness, feelings whose expression often comes through crying. However, they may have grown up hearing "big boys don't cry," or "only sissies cry," so they learn to suppress tears and often cover up their sadness and express anger instead of grief.

   • Similarly, many women have learned to suppress their anger. They may have been taught that raising their voice or becoming confrontational is inappropriate—the actions of a "bitch." So, instead of raising her voice or directly confronting a situation or person that angers her, a woman may instead become sad, covering her anger with tears.

   • Of course, we as men and women have many different ways of covering up our true feelings—of putting on facades or masks our gender socialization has taught us to present to others and ourselves.

   • A mask is a role, a behavior, or a way we act or present ourselves to others which disguises what we truly feel or think. Sometimes we get so good at it we don't even realize we are wearing a mask.

2. Distribute the **Gender Masks I Wear** worksheet and allow participants 10 minutes to complete it.

   ☞ *Some groups or individuals may have difficulty identifying some of their gender masks or may not even know how to describe or define the masks they wear. If this is the case, have the group brainstorm some masks men and women often wear to help each other get started.*

3. When they have completed the worksheet, have them select one mask (perhaps the one they present most often), and construct it.

   ☞ *Distribute the paper bags, magic markers, and other art supplies. The masks should be a visual or symbolic representation of how each sees his or her facade.*

4. When all have finished their masks, tell the participants to don their masks and move about the room interacting with one other. As soon as

they have had time to encounter almost everyone, ask each participant to sit down with a person of the gender they usually wear their mask for.

5. While keeping their masks on, instruct the pairs to spend 5 minutes having a conversation as they normally would.

6. Then have the pairs take off the masks and discuss their masked conversation using these reflection questions:

   ☞ *Put these questions on an easel chart where all can see them. You may want to circulate through the room to "listen in" on the process and help any pair who needs it.*

   ✔ Is the mask a safe, secure place to be?

   ✔ What parts of yourself are you hiding when you wear the mask?

   ✔ How do you feel about yourself when you wear the mask?

   ✔ How did it feel to talk to another mask?

7. After 10 minutes ask the participants to choose a new partner of the same gender as their previous partner and discuss something they would not usually say or would feel awkward or hesitant revealing about themselves.

8. Allow pairs 10 minutes to discuss their unmasked conversations using these questions:

   ☞ *Write the questions on an easel chart.*

   ✔ What did you feel during the conversation?

   ✔ What was different about this conversation than your masked conversation?

   ✔ What usually prevents you from interacting without your facade?

   ✔ Would you like to change this? If so, what new decisions would you have to make? How would you go about doing this?

9. Reconvene the entire group and allow each person an opportunity to show and describe their mask and to share anything they learned during the experience.

Activity 3: Common Gender Masks

1. Distribute the **Common Gender Masks** worksheets and ask participants to discuss them using the following questions:

   ☞ *Prior to the exercise, prepare an easel chart duplicating the worksheet and display it at this time.*

✔ Do any of our masks display characteristics found on the worksheet?

✔ Besides the mask you constructed, what other masks do you find yourself wearing?

✔ Which of these masks would you like to give up? What new behavior would this require?

✔ Do you think there is a correlation between wearing these gender masks and having low self-esteem?

☞ *A correlation does exist—the higher one's self-esteem, the less obliged he or she feels to wear masks.*

2. Encourage participants to take their masks off during the rest of the workshop to experience what it feels like to always be yourself.

VARIATIONS

■ In Activity 1, *Step 4*, provide more time for the entire group to interact while wearing their masks. Then use the discussion questions in *Step 6*. Conduct *Step 7* in the entire group.

■ If the group is having difficulty filling out the **Gender Masks I Wear** worksheet and brainstorming is not fruitful, distribute and discuss the **Common Gender Masks** worksheet before they start the first activity.

©1995 Whole Person Press 210 W Michigan Duluth MN 55802   (800) 247-6789

GENDER MASKS I WEAR

Directions: Identify the gender masks you wear in front of others to hide what you truly feel or think. Under "Mask," name the mask (anger, sorrow, dependency, aggressiveness) and describe how you act while wearing it; under "To hide or repress" record what you are trying to disguise; and check "M" (men), "W" (women), or both under the "in front of" column to indicate to which gender you tend to show this facade.

Mask:	To hide or repress:	In front of M W

COMMON GENDER MASKS

Male Gender Masks

1. Competitiveness, especially with other men

2. Aggression and domination (to hide being needy or dependent)

3. Inflexibility (to hide uncertainty, fear)

4. Dogmatism (arrogant, knows everything, acts superior, unwilling to show any weakness)

5. Homophobia

6. Distance from any "feminine" quality, out of touch with feelings like tenderness, vulnerability, sadness, grief, nurturing, and caring.

7. Anger (showing anger when you may really feel sad or confused)

8. Cruelty and violence (blaming others rather than dealing with your own feelings such as fear, weakness, resentment, etc.)

9. Sexual aggression (even though you may not really feel like initiating intimacy)

Female Gender Masks

1. Dependency

2. Self-blame or self-criticism (when responsibility is equally shared or belongs elsewhere)

3. Submissiveness (unwilling to show own strength)

4. Need for approval (especially from males)

5. Tears or depression (often hiding anger)

6. Acting dumb or inferior (especially around men)

7. Peacemaker (at any cost avoiding conflict)

8. Using sexuality (to get what you want instead of saying directly what you want, even though you may not wish to be intimate)

©1995 Whole Person Press 210 W Michigan Duluth MN 55802 (800) 247-6789

13 REVERSE EXPERIENCES

In this fun exercise, participants of each gender design role simulations for the other gender in order for men to experience a situation common to the women's lives and vice versa.

GOALS

To increase understanding of how the other gender feels in various situations.

To experience difficult situations the other gender may encounter simply because of their gender.

GROUP SIZE

Unlimited.

TIME

2 hours.

MATERIALS

Easels and easel paper; magic markers; masking tape.

PROCESS

1. Introduce the exercise by explaining that it will help participants better understand what it's like to be a member of the other gender.

2. Divide each gender group into teams of 4–6 participants and provide the following instructions:

   ➤ Each group will design a 5 minute role play experience for the other gender.

   ➤ The role play should help participants and observers better understand how it sometimes feels to be a member of the other gender.

   ➤ First, decide on the feeling or behavior your group wants the other group to experience.

   ☞ *For example, the women might decide to help men understand how it feels to be ignored in a meeting or to always have their bodies looked at and evaluated. The men might want to have the women learn how it feels to be expected to be fierce competitors.*

©1995 Whole Person Press 210 W Michigan Duluth MN 55802   (800) 247-6789

➤ It is important for each group to be clear as to the feelings or behavior you want the other group to discover.

➤ One of the other gender groups will participate in the simulation role play you develop.

➤ You will have 30 minutes to develop your role play.

☞ *If participants have little experience role-playing, a facilitator should join each group to help them develop their role play. While they are still developing their role plays, assign each group to role-play another group's simulation and write the pairings on a chart.*

3. After 30 minutes, call time and reconvene the entire group.

4. Have groups conduct each simulation with their paired other-gender group and use the following procedure to conduct a debriefing session after each role play:

   a. First, allow time for those in the role play to ventilate their feelings and share what they learned about being a member of the other gender.

   b. Ask observers what they saw and felt.

   c. Have the group who designed the simulation explain what feelings or behavior they wanted the other group to experience and why.

5. When all the role plays have been dramatized, provide an opportunity for participants to discuss what they learned.

☞ *Record these ideas on an easel chart.*

14 RELATIONSHIPS & FEEDBACK

Participants identify and discuss the kind of relationships they would like to have with one another.

GOALS

To give and receive feedback about relationships in the group.

To examine what gender role expectations we unconsciously hold of each other.

GROUP SIZE

10–20 participants.

TIME

$2^1/_2$ hours.

MATERIALS

Easels and easel paper; magic markers; masking tape; **Interaction Chart** worksheet.

PROCESS

☞ *Although it can be used as a first impressions activity, this exercise works best if people have already spent some time together.*

Activity 1: Individual Reflection

1. Introduce the activity by explaining that they will use a unique way to give and receive feedback.

2. Distribute the **Interaction Chart** worksheets and provide the following instructions:

   ☞ *If you have 12 or more participants, form several small mixed-gender groups*

   ➤ The worksheet contains different categories of relationships or types of interactions you may have had with other members of this group.

   ➤ Decide who in the group best fits each of the categories and write their name on the appropriate line.

☞ *If you have formed small groups, tell them to choose only people from their group.*

➤ Write only one name for each item.

➤ You may use the same name more than once.

☞ *There may be some initial reluctance. Encourage participants to take some risks and assure them they will learn a lot from participating.*

You have five minutes to complete the worksheet. Begin.

☞ *While they are working individually, prepare a chart with the worksheet categories on the left-hand side and participants' names across the top of the chart.*

3. After 5 minutes call time and ask the group to share their answers using the following procedure:

a. Starting with the first category, call out each participants's name and have the other participants raise their hands if they checked that person.

b. Place a check mark in the person's box for each participant who raises their hand.

c. Repeat until you have finished each category and each participant.

Activity 2: Interactive Feedback

1. Allow time for participants to examine the chart.

2. Ask for a volunteer to gather more information about why people identified him or her in specific categories. Follow this process:

a. Have the volunteer share how he or she is feeling about the feedback.

b. Invite the volunteer to ask questions and ask for additional feedback.

c. Ask them questions such as:

✔ What surprises and disappoints you about where your colleagues identified you?

✔ Does the feedback fit your gender role identity?

✔ Is there any place you would like to see more checks in the future?

3. Continue until all have a chance to receive additional feedback and share their feelings.

Activity 3: Gender Awareness / Stereotypes

1. Use the following questions to initiate a discussion about the gender patterns in the feedback chart.

    ✔ Do women's names appear more frequently than men's names in some categories?

    ✔ Are women's names missing in some categories?

    ✔ Does this fit the stereotypes of what we expect from women?

    ✔ Do men's names appear more frequently than women's names in some categories?

    ✔ Are men's names missing in some areas?

    ✔ Does this indicate gender stereotyping?

    ✔ What other gender themes seem to have emerged?

    ✔ What does this say about us as men and women?

2. End by having each participant answer two questions:

    ✔ What gender stereotypes do you hold about other men and women?

    ✔ What have you learned about yourself?

VARIATION

■ For another, more confidential way to chart the information, have participants put their names on their papers and hand them in for you to use to chart the information. Give them a break while you are charting the names.

INTERACTION CHART

Who would I like to have:

1. On a work team with me _____

2. As my boss _____

3. Support me in a personal crisis _____

4. As a best friend _____

Who do I feel:

1. Competitive with _____

2. Most in conflict with _____

3. Wants to be in the limelight the most _____

4. The most respect for _____

5. Listens the most _____

6. Attracted to _____

15 POSITIVES AND NEGATIVES

Participants identify past "turn offs" and "turn ons" and share specific things they like and dislike about men and women.

GOALS

To become aware of what we like and dislike about each gender.

To practice sharing our positive and negative impressions.

To learn how each person has affected others.

GROUP SIZE

10–25 participants (most effective with an ongoing group).

TIME

3 hours.

MATERIALS

Pencils; **Positives & Negatives** worksheet.

PROCESS

Activity 1: Self-Reflection

1. Briefly introduce the exercise with a chalktalk based on the following points:
   - Most of us usually have strong feelings about what we like and don't like about men and women.
   - These "turn ons" and "turn offs" may be based on several influences:
     - Past experiences in our adult relationships
     - Stereotypes and prescripts we learned from society
     - Past experiences as a child, especially with parents
   - Regardless of where they came from, these feelings unconsciously influence our communication and relationships with others.
   - Today we are going to become more conscious about these feelings and attitudes, exploring how they have affected our relationships in this group.

©1995 Whole Person Press 210 W Michigan Duluth MN 55802   (800) 247-6789

2. Distribute the **Positives & Negatives** worksheet and provide the following instructions:

➤ This worksheet will help you reflect on past "turn ons" and "turn offs."

➤ On the top half of the worksheet, make two lists: one of what you usually like or find positive about women and the other of what you often find annoying or negative about women.

➤ On the bottom half of the worksheet, make two similar lists, this time about men.

➤ You have ten minutes. Begin.

3. After 10 minutes ask participants to stop writing and put their worksheets aside.

Activity 2: Gender Sharing

1. Form two circles—one inner and the other outer—so that pairs of people face one another, and provide the following instructions:

☞ *Each circle should have a mix of women and men.*

➤ The participant in the inner circle is "Partner A;" the participant in the outer circle is "Partner B."

➤ Partner A tells Partner B what specific aspects of B's appearance, behavior, or personality has affected Partner A positively.

➤ Partner B does not respond verbally, but only listens.

➤ Partner A asks Partner B if he or she would like to hear a reservation, something about his or her appearance, behavior, or personality that Partner A finds annoying or negative and may prevent the two from becoming closer.

➤ Reservations should not be an insult or a criticism, rather they should provide information about where Partner A stands in relation to Partner B.

➤ If you receive permission to offer your reservation, do so as specifically as possible.

➤ Again, Partner B does not to respond verbally, but only listens.

➤ Reverse roles and repeat the procedure.

➤ I will call time after about 4 minutes and the outer circle will then move one person to the left.

➤ You will then repeat the process with your new partner.

©1995 Whole Person Press 210 W Michigan Duluth MN 55802   (800) 247-6789

☞ *Continue until the circle has gone all the way around to the original pair. You may wish to pair up with another facilitator and demonstrate the activity before beginning. If there is only one facilitator, ask for a volunteer to work with you.*

2. When the process is complete, have participants look again at their worksheet and privately compare it with the experience they just had.

3. Form mixed-gender groups of 6–8 participants to discuss the experience using the following questions:

   ✔ How do you feel about the feedback you were given?

   ✔ Did you get similar or different feedback from men and women?

   ✔ What did you learn about how other men and women see you?

   ✔ How comfortable were you giving feedback? Did your comfort level change depending on your partner's gender?

   ✔ What is the relationship between your past likes and dislikes and the present feedback you gave?

4. After 30 minutes, reconvene the entire group and ask them to share any insights they gained during the activity.

VARIATIONS

■ If time permits and the group is energized, conduct another round of the rotating pairs exercise so they can pair off with participants they have not yet been with.

■ If you want Activity 2 to focus more on male/female relationships, include only men in the inner circle and women in the outer. You could then have them meet in separate gender groups and take turns giving the same type of feedback to each participant of their own gender.

©1995 Whole Person Press 210 W Michigan Duluth MN 55802   (800) 247-6789

POSITIVES & NEGATIVES

What I like about women	What I dislike about women

What I like about men	What I dislike about men

16 GENDER FEEDBACK

In this stimulating exercise, participants give one another specific gender feedback that leads to productive discussion and insights.

GOALS

To give and receive gender feedback.

To discover if our self-image is congruent with how the other gender sees us.

GROUP SIZE

10–20 participants; most effective if gender groups can be divided equally.

TIME

3 hours.

MATERIALS

Easels and easel paper; magic markers; masking tape; **Self-Descriptions** worksheet.

PROCESS

Activity 1: Self-Descriptions

1. Distribute the worksheets and provide the following instructions:

    ➤ Think about yourself as a person of your gender. What are your assets and your areas for growth?

    ➤ Use the space under "How I See Myself" to write a physical and personality description of yourself.

    ➤ When you have finished, use the bottom half of the worksheet to describe how you think the other gender sees you.

2. After about 10 minutes, call time and tell participants to keep the worksheet for a later activity, but do nothing else with it for the moment.

©1995 Whole Person Press 210 W Michigan Duluth MN 55802   (800) 247-6789

Activity 2: Gender Feedback

1. Separate participants into same-gender groups and have them move to separate rooms.

2. Provide each gender group with the following instructions:

   ➤ We are going to consider each person from the other group and discuss how we see her [him] as a woman [man].

   ➤ Be as specific with your feedback as possible.

      ☞ *You may want to present feedback guidelines before starting this activity (descriptive, behavioral, specific, etc.).*

   ➤ We will record the feedback on an easel sheet for that person.

      ☞ *Record all feedback on the easel sheet—there does not have to be group consensus on any item. Do not put the name of the person who is being discussed on the sheet. Each group may want to place a secret code on each easel sheet to help them remember who it is about.*

      You may need to talk about how they are feeling about the task before proceeding—they may be reluctant to participate or feel anxious about it. Let them share their feelings and then try to encourage them to give it a try.

3. Start the activity and continue until your group has created a feedback sheet for everyone in the other group, including facilitators.

4. Reconvene the entire group, ask the gender groups to post the feedback sheets, then have the entire group follow this process:

   ➤ Individually read the feedback sheets and try to identify your own.

   ➤ When you think you have found your sheet, write your name on it.

   ➤ More than one person can claim the same feedback sheet.

5. When all have placed their names on a sheet, have each gender group inform the other which sheet belongs to whom.

6. Give them a minute to read their sheet and compare it to their worksheet.

7. Allow each participant time to ask for clarification of the feedback and to share his or her feelings. Encourage them to ask questions about their sheet and process the feedback with the following questions:

   ✔ How do you feel about your feedback sheet?

✔ Does anything surprise you? If so, what?

✔ Does the feedback agree with how you believe others see you?

✔ Does the feedback agree with how you described yourself on your worksheet?

8. Encourage participants to identify any common patterns, perceptions, or stereotypes they noticed on the feedback sheets.

9. Close by inviting participants to share what they learned or experienced during this exercise.

VARIATIONS

■ If time permits, in *Step 7* of Activity 2, allow time for participants to request feedback from their gender group to determine if people of their own gender have the same perceptions about them as do people of the other gender.

■ This exercise can lead to intensive discussions about stereotyping and gender roles. For example, men sometimes provide more feedback about the physical aspects of women than any other trait. If time permits, spend time examining what this feedback and other similar role stereotyping feedback might mean in terms of gender prescripts. This makes the exercise an even more worthwhile learning experience.

■ Instead of discussing the feedback in gender groups, post one easel sheet for each member of the other gender group and have each group member write his or her feedback on each.

SELF-DESCRIPTIONS

How I see myself

How I think the other gender sees me

17 HOW FAR DO I HAVE TO GO?

Participants give one another specific gender role attitude and behavior feedback and develop action plans based on the feedback.

GOALS

To give and receive feedback about our gender role attitudes and behavior.

To develop action plans for self-growth concerning gender issues.

GROUP SIZE

10–20 participants (most effective with an ongoing group).

TIME

3 hours.

MATERIALS

Pencils and pens; **Gender Role Feedback** worksheet.

PROCESS

☞ *It is important to conduct this module near the end of the workshop in order for participants to have observed behavior and attitudes in one another. This makes an excellent concluding exercise.*

Activity 1: Individual Feedback

1. Introduce the issue of gender feedback by making the following points:

   • During your time together as a group you have had opportunities to observe how each person expresses attitudes about gender issues and gender behavior.

   • Today you will give each other feedback about those attitudes and behaviors.

2. Distribute the worksheet and provide the following instructions:

   ➤ You are going to rate each individual on a gender role stereotyping scale.

☞ *Read the information on the worksheet that explains the numbers on the scale and provide examples wherever appropriate.*

➤ You must rate each individual in the group, including yourself.

➤ Base your rating on behavior and attitudes you have witnessed during our time together.

➤ Be honest and open.

➤ You will have 20 minutes to work on this feedback. Begin.

☞ *While they are working, prepare an easel chart with each person's name and a scale next to it.*

3. After 20 minutes, or when all have finished, ask them to chart their feedback on the easel chart by placing a check with their initials next to where they rated each individual.

Activity 2: Group Feedback

1. Ask individuals to examine their feedback charts.

2. Allow time for each person to discuss the feedback with the group, encouraging them to:

   • share their initial reactions and feelings.

   • ask for additional information about why they were given the various ratings.

   • discuss ways they would like to change and how they could begin making those changes.

3. End by having each individual share how they felt during this activity.

VARIATION

■ Custom design the gender role scale to each particular group. For example, if conducting a workshop for married couples, use unequal or equal gender relationships in the marriage; for a work group, use gender relationships in the workplace.

©1995 Whole Person Press 210 W Michigan Duluth MN 55802   (800) 247-6789

GENDER ROLE FEEDBACK

Gender Role Scale

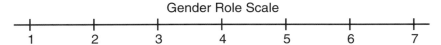

1–2 Views men as superior to women; believes men should be dominant, women submissive; contemptuous or patronizing of the
other gender; quick to criticize the other gender; believes in and
practices double standards; highly-internalized sexism or sexism.

6–7 Views men and women as equals; practices equality; very open to
examining own sexism or internalized sexism; practices mutual
empowerment and empathy; believes in shared responsibility.

Name	Rating	Specific Behavior/Attitudes

©1995 Whole Person Press 210 W Michigan Duluth MN 55802   (800) 247-6789

TRAINER'S NOTES

Women and Men
as Colleagues

WOMEN AND MEN AS COLLEAGUES

25 GENDER QUIZ   (p 101)

In this fun, "game show" exercise, participants answer questions about gender behavior as they learn new information about communication between genders. (1$\frac{1}{2}$ hours)

26 SEXISM   (p 106)

Using worksheet examples, male participants share and discuss their sexism and women participants their internalized sexism. (2—2$\frac{1}{2}$ hours)

27 HOMOPHOBIA AND SEXISM   (p 111)

By dispelling myths with facts, this exercise examines homophobia, its parallels to sexism, and its effect on the workplace. (2—3 hours)

28 IF I WOKE UP TOMMORROW AS   (p 116)

In an effort to better understand their colleagues, participants imagine how their lives would change if they woke up the next day as the other gender. (2 hours)

29 LEADING AND FOLLOWING   (p 120)

Men lead women and women lead men in order to explore how genders respond to and interact with one another in supervisory and subordinate roles. (1$\frac{1}{2}$ hours)

30 LANGUAGE   (p 123)

Participants explore the effect language has on gender attitudes and self image and learn how to eliminate gender bias in communications. (1$\frac{1}{2}$ hours)

31 DOUBLE STANDARDS   (p 131)

Participants explore how certain work behavior is sometimes viewed differently depending on whether a man or woman exhibited the behavior. Makes a great follow-up exercise to Exercise 30. (1$\frac{1}{2}$ hours)

32 GROUP GENDER DYNAMICS   (p 134)

Participants develop a vision of a gender-bias free world and observe the gender dynamics of a work group. (2$\frac{1}{2}$ hours)

33 LEADERSHIP STYLES   (p 139)

Designed for managers and supervisors, this exercise helps participants understand typical male and female leadership styles as well as their own and those of their colleagues. ($2\frac{1}{2}$ hours)

34 GENDER SCENARIOS   (p 144)

Participants use role plays to examine how to effectively handle workplace gender issues that concern them. (2—3 hours)

35 GENDER PERCEPTIONS   (p 148)

Designed for colleagues in the same organization, this exercise helps participants gain a better understanding of one another by identifying the type of gender bias men and women experience in the workplace. (2 hours)

36 GENDER MIRRORS   (p 150)

Participants share how they view the other gender, identify gender problems, and develop action plans to solve them—another exercise designed specifically for men and women who work together.(3—4 hours)

37 GENDER SUPPORT (p 153)

Participants in the same organization identify ways they can support each other and identify behavior changes they need the other gender to make to help them be more successful and productive. Makes a great ending to a workshop. (3 hours)

OVERVIEW

As more and more women have entered the work force, the process of men and women working together has helped to eliminate gender stereotypes and prejudices—yet at the same time it has created tension, confusion, resentment, and misunderstanding between men and women who work as colleagues.

While women now occupy entry- and middle-level positions, few have gained entrance to the executive suite. Today men and women compete for many of the same jobs—a fact many men resent—especially as organizations eliminate jobs and positions in an effort to downsize. Organizational barriers blocking women from moving into jobs traditionally seen as "man's work" still exist. Because of this, most companies suffer gender discrimination problems that affect their profitability.

At the same time, many Americans have become disillusioned with corporate life. Some, particularly women, have walked away from the traditional corporate world to start their own businesses. Men have begun to redefine themselves and reevaluate what it means to be a successful man both on the job and in the home; they have started to demand, as many women have, both a challenging career and time to be involved parents. These changes force companies who want to attract and retain valuable employees to address such issues as family care and discrimination against women (as well as racism, heterosexism, and ethnocentrism.)

Socialization has created communication problems among both genders. Employees bring society's gender stereotypes and gender role prescripts to the workplace, adversely affecting women's careers. For example, supervisors often evaluate a woman's performance with different standards than they use for a man's. In addition, the old social rules of conduct (opening doors, pulling out chairs, modifying vocabulary, treating women as sex objects, etc.) have been recognized as incorrect, adding to the tension between women and men.

Socialization has also forced women to face double standards on the job—not just from men but from some women who have received and accepted the same negative socialization messages about women and work as their male counterparts. While many men fully support the advances made by the women they work with, male resistance to equality has increased in some organizations. Some men feel women have made major progress and have even enjoyed an advantage because of sexual favoritism or affirmative action, despite statistics to the contrary (a notion that devalues women's hard work and achievement). Even some women, unaware of their own internalized sexism, may contribute to the perpetuation of inequity by underestimating the impact of gender discrimination on their careers, believing they are immune from discrimination or blaming other women for not being "good enough." Women may also resist examining and dealing with their own racism, heterosexism, and other biases.

Organizations should offer training sessions in which women and men can learn to communicate directly and become more aware of gender-based assumptions and attitudes—groups with the goal of altering relationships between women and men in order to create mutual respect. This kind of training also encourages a new kind of male-female camaraderie at work.

The exercises in this section help trainers create successful workplace gender workshops. Keep in mind the importance of having both female and male facilitators lead the group sessions as a team, sharing responsibility equally. Facilitators working together provide role models for participants. Facilitators must understand and be able to identify group gender dynamics, such as the different roles men and women assume during group discussions (for example, women often do more supporting, listening, and reflecting, while men tend to become challenging or take on problem solving tasks). Facilitators should have an awareness of their own prejudices and be open to self-examination. They should also be comfortable working with resistance.

The exercises in this section are designed for the business environment and can be used in a one day to week-long training session. Start with less threatening exercises and move to ones that require more self-disclosure and communication between genders. Earlier exercises provide time in same-gender groups, the starting point for gender growth. Choose the exercises that best fit your participants and their organizational climate.

18 GENDER STEREOTYPES

This exercise allows participants to acknowledge their gender biases and provides them with an opportunity to discuss common gender stereotypes.

GOALS

To identify gender stereotypes.

To begin to understand that everyone has learned to be biased about men and women.

To recognize how gender preconceptions have perfused society.

GROUP SIZE

Unlimited.

TIME

$1^{1}/_{2}$ hours.

MATERIALS

Easel paper; magic markers; masking tape; pens and pencils; **Gender Stereotypes** worksheet.

PROCESS

☞ *Decide which stereotypes you want to use prior to the exercise, write each on a separate easel sheet of paper, and post the sheets on the walls throughout the room. Cover up each sheet so participants can't read them. Suggested groups include: women, men; feminists, macho men; passive women, aggressive men; sexual harassers, women who file sexual harassment complaints; old women, old men; young women, young men; married men, married women; single men, single women; lesbians, gays; sexually active women, sexually active men; women of color, men of color; white women, white men; and women managers, men managers. Make sure to include both men and women for each category you include.*

Activity 1: Stereotype Identification

1. Distribute worksheets and provide the following instructions:

➤ We are going to examine the stereotypes associated with gender groups in the United States.

➤ I will ask you to identify stereotypes you know exist in this culture about certain gender groups—not necessarily stereotypes you hold or believe, but those you know exist.

➤ Whenever I name a group, write its name on one of the blank lines and then list the stereotypes you know some people associate with that particular group beneath its name.

☞ *As you name a group, reveal its easel sheet.*

➤ Do not censor yourself. You will be using the information in the next part of the exercise, but no one else will see your worksheet.

2. After you have finished *Step 1*, ask participants to write the stereotypes they listed on the appropriate easel sheets following these directions:

➤ Do not repeat stereotypes others have listed.

➤ Our emphasis is on quantity; we are trying to list every stereotype associated with each group.

➤ Be honest and candid.

3. When all have finished, ask one participant to read aloud the stereotypes listed for the first group.

☞ *Continue having participants take turns reading the stereotypes for the group. Make sure a participant does not have to read stereotypes about a group they belong to; for example, an African-American woman should not read stereotypes listed for women of color.*

Activity 2: Impact of Gender Stereotypes

1. Form mixed-gender groups of 6 participants and move to separate spaces in the room.

2. Have participants use the questions below to discuss their reactions to the first activity:

✔ What gender groups do you identify with and what did you feel as we read the stereotype lists for those groups?

✔ Where do we learn these stereotypes?

✔ How do they impact your behavior at work?

✔ What can you do to avoid having these stereotypes influence your behavior at work?

✔ Do you ever hear stereotypical gender comments at work? What are they?

✔ Do you ever hear stereotypical gender comments in your personal life? What are they?

✔ How can you effectively respond to these comments?

3. After about 30 minutes, reconvene the entire group and ask each group to share highlights from their discussions; in particular, ask for ways the groups came up with to avoid having stereotypes influence their behavior at work and to effectively respond to stereotypical comments.

4. Encourage participants to continue to explore and consider what gender stereotypes they hold as they participate in the remaining workshop exercises.

VARIATION

■ If time is limited, skip using the worksheets and move directly to the easel sheets.

GENDER STEREOTYPES

Group: _____   Group: _____   Group: _____

Group: _____   Group: _____   Group: _____

Group: _____   Group: _____   Group: _____

Group: _____   Group: _____   Group: _____

Group: _____   Group: _____   Group: _____

19 GENDER ATTITUDES

This introductory exercise finds participants sharing their gender attitudes and experiences in order to build trust and get to know one another on a different level.

GOALS

To encourage participants to talk openly.

To build group trust.

To discover participants' gender attitudes.

GROUP SIZE

15–30 (most effective with an equal number of men and women).

TIME

2 hours.

MATERIALS

None.

PROCESS

Activity 1: Rotating Pairs

☞ *Create 2 circles of chairs facing one another so participants face one another in pairs when seated.*

1. State the exercise's goals, ask one gender group to sit in the inner circle of chairs and the other to sit in the outer circle, and provide the following instructions:.

   ☞ *Each participant should now face a partner of the other gender. If there is an uneven number of men and women, have some of the facilitators participate. It does not matter which gender sits in which circle. No matter how you set up the circles, one of the participants will invariably ask why X gender was in X circle.*

   ➤ You and your partner have 5 minutes to share how you would complete an open-ended sentence I will provide for you.

   ➤ Sentences will be about both men and women, so reply to both.

➤ There are no right or wrong answers so don't censor yourself; share the first thought that comes to your mind.

➤ After 5 minutes, you will shift to a new partner, and I will give you a new open-ended sentence.

2. Read an open-ended sentence from the Gender Attitudes Open-Ended Sentences list.

    ☞ *Choose a progression of questions starting with less threatening ones and ending with those requiring a higher level of risk.*

3. After 5 minutes, instruct participants in the outer circle to move one person to his or her right.

4. Repeat *Steps 2* and *3* until the outer circle has talked with everyone in the inner circle (or, if time is short, until they have talked with at least 10 other participants).

Activity 2: Gender Attitude Discussion

1. Create same-gender groups and lead a discussion using the following questions:

    ✔ How did you feel while participating in this exercise?

    ✔ Where you comfortable? Why or when?

    ✔ Where you ever uncomfortable? Why or when?

        ☞ *Men are sometimes uncomfortable completing Sentence 6 and some may skip it. This is a good opportunity to begin a discussion of homophobia.*

    ✔ When were you honest?

    ✔ When did you hold back?

    ✔ Did you notice any patterns of or differences between the male and female responses? If so, what? How do you feel about this?

    ✔ Did any responses surprise you? If so, what?

2. Reconvene the entire group and have participants share some of their reactions to the first activity.

    ☞ *Often men will hold back more than women and seem to be less honest in some of their responses. If the women perceive dishonesty, encourage them to share their perceptions with the men. This sharing can open up some excellent dialogue.*

VARIATIONS

■ Instead of using the suggested open-ended sentences, make up your own that are custom tailored to your group.

Gender Attitudes Open-Ended Sentences

☞ *Remind participants to complete sentences containing text within brackets [] twice, once for each gender.*

1. In school I learned that important women [men] in history were . . . and that gave me the message that women [men] are . . .

2. Toys, games, and activities I was given or encouraged to play with (not given or allowed to play with) were . . . and that gave me the message that I could (could not) . . .

3. Growing up, my father (or father figure) [mother (or mother figure)] acted in the following ways . . . and that gave me the message that men [women] should . . .

4. What I don't understand or what confuses me the most about my own gender [the other gender] is . . .

5. Emotions I am generally comfortable [uncomfortable] expressing around persons of the other gender include . . . and emotions I am comfortable [uncomfortable] with the other gender expressing are . . .

6. An attractive woman [man] to me is . . .

7. When I'm with men [women] I sometimes hold back or pretend . . .

8. At work I think men [women] often see and respond to women [men] in the following ways . . .

9. Women [men] annoy me when they . . .

10. Sex and sexuality for most men [women] is . . .

11. If I woke up tomorrow and found myself the other gender, my life would be different in the following ways . . .

12. At work I think men [women] often see me as . . .

13. Offer the following feedback to your partner: My impression of you as a man [woman] is . . .

20 GENDER ISSUES

In this introductory exercise, participants engage in a fun, nonthreatening activity to begin identifying gender issues.

GOALS

To begin identifying gender issues in the workplace.

To prepare to discuss gender issues without being defensive.

GROUP SIZE

15–30 participants.

TIME

$1^1/_2$ hours.

MATERIALS

Easel chart and easel paper; pencils and pens; pillows (about 20).

PROCESS

Activity 1: Gender Reversal

1. Use the following points to introduce the exercise:

   • This session will focus on gender issues in the workplace.

   • Even though the topic is serious, I think you're going to have fun with the activity.

   • At the very least, you'll find it a different way to learn about gender issues.

2. Ask the men to sit in a circle in the middle of the room, facing each other, and give them the following instructions:

   ☞ *If the group is dressed informally, have them sit on pillows to create a more informal atmosphere and make it easier for the outside group to listen to the inside circle.*

   ➤ Spend about 10 minutes discussing "the issues women have in this organization" as if you were women.

   ☞ *Post this task on the easel.*

©1995 Whole Person Press 210 W Michigan Duluth MN 55802   (800) 247-6789

➤ Don't change your voice or physical mannerisms; just identify issues you think women in the company are concerned with and talk about them in the way you think women would discuss them.

➤ The women are to listen, but may not comment or interrupt.

➤ Begin the discussion.

☞ *Facilitators should encourage, but not force, each man to contribute to the discussion. Allow silences.*

3. After about 10 minutes, thank the men for their participation, ask them to trade places with women, and give the women the following instructions:

➤ Hold a discussion about "the issues men have in this organization" as if you were men.

☞ *Post this task on the easel.*

➤ Don't change your voice or physical mannerisms; just identify issues you think men in the company are concerned with and talk about them in the way you think men would discuss them.

➤ The men are to listen, but may not comment or interrupt.

➤ Begin the discussion.

☞ *Again, facilitators should encourage, but not force, each woman to contribute to the discussion. Allow silences.*

4. After about 10 minutes call time and reconvene the entire group.

Activity 2: Reversal Discussion

1. Invite the men to share their feelings about how easy or difficult it was for them to identify and discuss issues they think women might have.

2. Ask the women to share their perceptions of how accurate the men were, especially what was really on target and what was missed.

3. Invite the women to share their feelings about how easy or difficult it was for them to identify and discuss issues they think men might have.

4. Ask the men to share their perceptions of how accurate the women were, especially what was really on target and what was missed.

☞ *In Steps 1 and 3, some participants may mention that they didn't really have any idea what issues might concern the other gender and have never taken the time to think about them or listen to the other gender discuss them.*

©1995 Whole Person Press 210 W Michigan Duluth MN 55802 (800) 247-6789

In Steps 2 and 4, some defensive participants may deny issues the other group came up with, particularly if that group was on target. One way to handle this is to ask to hear from others who may believe the issue was accurate. This helps some participants move beyond their denial.

Often both women and men will miss some of the more "vulnerable" issues men have, such as few close friends in the workplace or the competition they experience with other men. Use your own judgement whether to discuss issues they have not mentioned. If you plan on following this exercise with Exercise #21, you may want to wait until then to decide if your group is ready to discuss these issues.

5. End the exercise by thanking the participants for starting to take some risks in exploring gender issues.

21 INDIVIDUAL CONCERNS

This serious exercise helps participants examine the gender issues that exist in their workplace—an excellent exercise to combine with Exercise 20, **Gender Issues**.

GOALS

To provide an opportunity for participants to share their concerns about gender issues in the workplace.

To begin to understand each gender's concerns.

To identify concerns we share with same-gender colleagues.

GROUP SIZE

Unlimited (but requires a facilitator for each group of 8–10 participants).

TIME

$1^1/_2$ hours.

MATERIALS

Easel and easel paper; magic markers; masking tape; **Gender Concerns** worksheets.

PROCESS

Activity 1: Individual Issues

1. Introduce the exercise by explaining its goals.

2. Form mixed-gender groups of 8–10 participants; assign a facilitator to each group.

3. Distribute the worksheets, read the instructions, and give participants 2 minutes to fill them out.

4. When all have finished, ask participants to share their responses by following this process:

   a. Ask a participant to share one item on her or his list and discuss it with the group, giving specific examples of how the issue affects him or her.

b. Ask if anyone else of the first participant's gender also checked off that item and have them provide any additional examples or share their feelings about this issue.

c. Allow time for members of the other gender to ask questions about the item at hand.

d. Select a participant of the other gender and ask him or her to share an issue they checked off.

e. Repeat *Steps a–d* until all the issues have been discussed.

☞ *As a facilitator, keep a tally of which items were checked and by how many. Also be aware that some men find it difficult to admit that certain issues (such as competition and having few close friends) affect them and also find it difficult to share their concerns with others. It is helpful if male facilitators raise these concerns first and give positive reinforcement to men who voice them.*

Activity 2: Gender Concerns

1. After about 1 hour, reconvene the entire group and have facilitators report the central issues their groups listed.

   ☞ *Record these on an easel.*

2. Initiate a brief discussion on the key issues listed for both genders.

3. Invite the women to share what they learned from participating in this exercise, what they may need to do in the future to have their concerns addressed, and what could they do to help resolve the men's concerns.

4. Invite the men to share what they learned from participating in this exercise, what they may need to do in the future to have their concerns addressed, and what could they do to help resolve the women's concerns.

5. Ask participants what they think their discussion may mean for the organization—how they think these concerns impact employees, managers, and the organization as a whole.

6. Encourage participants to share any other insights.

7. Thank participants for their insights and encourage them to take actions to help resolve their concerns.

VARIATIONS

■ If you have fewer than 15 participants do not form small groups in Activity 1.

■ If you have extra time, conduct *Step 1* of Activity 2 in separate gender groups to discuss what can be done about their own and the other gender's concerns; then have them report possible action steps in the entire group.

GENDER CONCERNS

Instructions: The lists below contain some gender concerns. Read the list of concerns that tend to be associated with your gender and check the concerns you share. Then read the other gender's list and check those that you are also concerned with. Finally, add any gender concerns of your own not found on either list.

Women's Concerns

❑   Receiving disrespect and patronizing remarks and attitudes from some male colleagues.

❑   Being paid less than men for the same work and feeling that they have to be better performers then men to get ahead or even to receive positive evaluations.

❑   Finding few or no opportunities for promotion to upper-management positions exist for women (the glass ceiling).

❑   Receiving less performance-based feedback and information on the job than men do and lacking sponsors or mentors.

❑   Being kept out of informal male networking and bonding activities (golf outings, men's clubs, etc.).

❑   Having their authority less readily accepted than that of a male colleague of equal stature.

❑   Being sexually harassed.

❑   Not being believed to be capable of performing certain tasks, especially traditional jobs associated with men.

❑   Finding themselves ignored in meetings or discussions.

❑   Being seen, especially by men, as hired or promoted because of Affirmative Action and not because of their own achievements.

❑   Receiving fewer training opportunities and being kept from certain assignments that would help advancement.

❑   Often having two full time jobs; in the workplace and in the home (house chores and parenting).

©1995 Whole Person Press 210 W Michigan Duluth MN 55802   (800) 247-6789

GENDER CONCERNS, continued

Men's Concerns

❑ Feeling pressure to provide the family's income. This includes feeling forced to stay in a disliked job.

❑ Feeling susceptible to stress-related illnesses that lead to a shorter life span.

❑ Needing a more balanced life, with family and career receiving equal attention.

❑ Suffering from "Workaholism"—being addicted to work.

❑ Confused about how to behave in the presence of women colleagues.

❑ Feeling like the "wrong" gender in today's world.

❑ Under pressure to perform—always having to have the answers and to be perfect employees.

❑ Having self-identity tied up with the job and fearing job loss or lack of promotions.

❑ Difficult to be involved fathers while maintaining income, prestige, and organizational support.

❑ Having only superficial relationships with other men and no or few close friends.

❑ Needing to compete with other men in work, sports, or social conversation.

_____

❑ _____

❑ _____

❑ _____

22 GENDER QUESTIONS

Participants generate questions about the other gender and then have their questions answered.

GOALS

To open communication between men and women in a nonthreatening and nonjudgmental way.

To increase understanding between men and women.

GROUP SIZE

10–20 participants.

TIME

2 hours.

MATERIALS

Easel and easel paper; magic markers; masking tape.

PROCESS:

Activity 1: Questions

1. Introduce the exercise with the following comments:
   - Most of us have questions about the other gender—why they think, feel, or act in certain ways.
   - Today we are going to explore those questions while keeping in mind there are no pat answers and not all members of the same gender will agree with any one response.

2. Form same-gender groups and present the following task:
   - ➤ Develop a list of questions you would like the other gender to answer.
   - ➤ Include questions you've always wondered about, even ones that may sound stupid or silly, and list them on easel paper.

3. Move the groups to separate rooms and give them 20 minutes to generate their questions.

4. Reconvene the entire group after 20 minutes and toss a coin to determine which group will ask their questions first.

   ☞ *Tape this group's questions on the wall.*

5. Share these rules with the group before starting:

   ☞ *Choose one participant to select a question and request replies from one or more individuals of the other group. When the question has been answered let another participant ask a question. Do not allow one person to always ask or answer the questions.*

   ➤ No one has to answer a question.

   ➤ There is to be no argument or rebuttal from the group asking the questions after a question is answered. However, if someone from the group answering disagrees with the person answering, he or she may register that response.

   ➤ The group being questioned has the option of asking their inquirer for his or her opinion of their reply.

   ➤ Anyone may ask for clarification if you do not understand the question or answer.

   ➤ The group has 30 minutes to ask their questions and receive answers.

   ➤ At the end of 30 minutes, I'll call time and let the other group have a turn. Begin.

6. After 30 minutes, repeat *Step 5* with the other group asking the questions.

Activity 2: Gender Group Reflection

1. Return participants to their same-gender groups and use the following questions to generate discussion:

   ✔ Did you learn anything about how the other gender feels or thinks? If so, what?

   ✔ Were there times when you disagreed or felt uncomfortable when someone of your own gender answered a question? If so, when? What did you feel at that time?

   ✔ Were any questions or responses especially upsetting to anyone? If so, which ones and why?

   ✔ Were there any questions you would like to learn more about or did not get answers to? What were they? How might you explore these further?

✔ Were you open and honest in your answers or did you hold back some thoughts or feelings you had? If you did hold back, what was preventing you from being more open?

✔ Were there any moments when you were worried or concerned about how members of the other gender were responding or feeling toward you or your group? What behavior did you exhibit at this time?

✔ As a result of this experience, what would you like to change in how you relate to the other gender?

2. Reconvene the entire group and ask them to form pairs with a member of the other gender to discuss what they learned or felt during this experience.

3. After 10 minutes, ask each pair to join with another, creating groups of 4, and continue to discuss their insights.

4. After 15 minutes, reconvene the entire group and give participants an opportunity to state any significant insights they gained during the exercise.

VARIATION

■ Instead of allowing 30 minutes for each gender group to ask all their questions at once, alternate the questioning between gender groups.

23 SOCIALIZATION MESSAGES

This exercise helps participants identify and explore gender messages and examine the effect these messages have had on their behavior and how they view the other gender.

GOALS

To identify gender role messages participants have received.

To begin examining how these messages have influenced individual behaviors and feelings.

To give participants an opportunity to understand one another better.

GROUP SIZE

10–30 participants (most effective if gender groups can be divided equally).

TIME

2¹/₂ hours.

MATERIALS

Easels and easel paper; magic markers; masking tape.

PROCESS

Activity 1: Introduction to Socialization Messages

1. Start with a chalktalk about gender socialization in our society, covering such points as:

    *   Socialization is pressure to conform to certain expected behaviors, attitudes, and values.

    *   Both men and women receive strong socialization messages which influence who we grow up to be and continue to be.

    *   We receive these messages from television, advertisements, movies, books, magazines, schools, religious institutions, peers, and our parents and other adults.

    *   We tend to live according to their prescripts because we start life wanting approval and affection, and we fear rejection.

    *   Women and men receive different sets of messages.

- The central messages men receive tell them they must be competitive, must be the primary breadwinners for their family, and are superior to women.

- Women's primary messages tell them they must look attractive, must have good relationship skills, and that they are "less than" men.

2. Ask the group for several other examples of gender socialization messages men and women receive.

3. Explain that the next activity will provide them with an opportunity to examine more specific messages they have received throughout life, particularly while growing up.

Activity 2: Socialization

1. Form same-gender groups, move them to separate meeting rooms, and give each group the following instructions:

   ☞ *Separate rooms are essential because working in the same room will inhibit participants.*

   ➤ We will identify and discuss messages we received about men, women, and sex, in that order.

   ➤ Remember, gender messages come from a variety of sources, from parents to media.

   ➤ This is not a consensus activity—any message someone has received will be valued and recorded on the easel chart.

2. Invite each participant to share messages he or she remembers receiving and record them on a easel chart.

   ☞ *Record the messages using the participants' own words. Do not edit or summarize them. Write full sentences, not just one word descriptions, which are often labels, not messages. Participants in either group may express concerns about what is going up on the chart, thinking about sharing the information with the other group. Men particularly may be concerned about being honest about the sex messages they received and may be reluctant to share messages about sex or may not claim ownership of their messages when the entire group is together. You may need to discuss anxieties about sharing explicit sexual messages with the other group. Sometimes it becomes necessary for facilitators to share some of their own explicit sex messages in order to get their group to be honest. Do not record messages if participants are not willing to claim ownership of them.*

3. Reconvene the entire group after about 1 hour or when both groups have had adequate time to create their lists.

4. Give the following instructions for the gender groups to share their lists:

   ➤ We will start with the men's messages about men.

   ➤ Each man will take a turn reading a message from their list.

   ➤ The women are to listen silently.

   ➤ When the men have finished sharing their list, the women may ask questions to clarify the messages.

   ➤ We will then repeat the process with the women sharing their messages about men.

5. Use the questions below to engage participants in a brief discussion about what influence these messages have had on them, especially in the workplace.

   ☞ *Switch genders referred to in the questions using the pronouns in brackets.*

   ✔ What similarities, differences, and major themes did you notice?

   ✔ How have these messages affected how men [women] see themselves?

   ✔ How have these messages affected how women [men] view and relate to men [women] in the workplace?

6. Repeat *Steps 4* and *5* but change the focus to messages about women, with the women sharing their messages first.

7. Again repeat *Steps 4* and *5* but change the focus to the messages about sex, having the men share their sexual messages first.

   ☞ *You will notice major differences between the sex messages women and men receive.*

   The rationale for including messages about sex is that they influence men's and women's attitudes about sexual harassment in the workplace, and you can use these lists again if you work on sexual harassment. Men are sometimes uneasy about having women see the messages they received about sex and it is important for the facilitators to give positive feedback to the men if they have shared some very explicit sexual messages. If they held back and did not put much on the sex charts, the women will probably express disappointment that the men did not take risks. It is important to allow this discussion, but keep it open to avoid defensiveness.

Activity 3: Message Impact

1. Once again separate participants into same-gender groups and have facilitators use the questions below to lead a discussion about how these messages affect their behavior in the workplace:

   ✔ What is a major effect these messages have on you and other women [men] in the workplace?

   ✔ What new insights do you have about how these messages influence the other gender's behavior?

   ✔ What healthier messages could we give ourselves?

   ✔ Which of the messages do you feel are positive?

   ✔ What corrective actions could you take to help overcome the destructive effects of some of these messages?

   ✔ What would you have to give up in order to change?

   ✔ What would you gain by changing?

2. Reconvene the entire group and allow time for each gender group to share what they discussed and discovered when they analyzed the gender messages they received.

3. Thank the participants for their openness and give positive feedback to those who offered thoughtful insights about the messages.

VARIATIONS

■ Follow this procedure as an alternative to Activity 1:

   1. Divide participants into same-gender groups and give them 10 minutes to draw pictures that illustrate some key gender messages they received from parents, peers, school, religion, and media.

   2. Have each individual share and explain his or her illustration.

   3. Encourage participants to discuss and identify key messages as they emerge.

   4. Reconvene the entire group and have each gender group share their messages and the effects they have had.

■ In *Step 2* of Activity 1, invite participants to close their eyes and call out messages they received about being male or female.

■ To show how healthier messages can be presented, especially to children, show parts of the video **Free to Be You and Me**. The video can be ordered through Ladyslipper Catalog, 1-800-634-6044.

24 THEMES AND MYTHS

In this chalktalk/assessment exercise, participants learn about the major themes of gender role messages and examine their overall affect.

GOALS

To better understand the major themes of gender socialization.

To identify the myths involved in our socialization.

To increase our understanding of how gender messages oppress both women and men.

GROUP SIZE

Unlimited.

TIME

$1^1/_2$ hours.

MATERIALS

Easel and easel paper; magic markers; masking tape; **Socialization Themes** worksheet.

PROCESS

☞ *This exercise should follow Exercise 7 and Exercise 23, the socialization message exercises.*

Activity 1: Gender Socialization Themes

Present a chalktalk about gender messages and how they oppress both women and men; make certain to mention the following points:

- Male role expectations include more positive and socially-valued characteristics than those for women, yet the attempt to conform to these male role expectations has negative consequences for men.
- The major themes in the socialization of men include:
  - ○ **Don't be a sissy.** Boys are expected to reject anything related to female behavior. They should not allow themselves to be vulnerable or express any vulnerable feelings. They should not allow themselves to get close to other boys.

○ **Be a big wheel.** The signs of importance include how much wealth, fame, or success you have achieved. Men feel pressure to compete with other men to achieve these external things and display their superiority. Personal and interpersonal fulfillment is not valued, and women may be used as symbols of success rather than life companions.

○ **Be self-reliant and go it alone**. Men are expected to give off an aura of confidence and unshakable strength. Whether they need medical care or directions, they should never ask for help. Show toughness at all times.

○ **Be a warrior in life.** Men should enjoy aggression and risk taking, always striving to be more powerful than others, even if it means violence. They should not be giving at any time.

• Men who buy into this socialization—and it's almost impossible not to to some degree—find themselves caught in a double bind. If a man goes along with these male prescripts, his basic human needs—such as to love and be loved, to find meaning and fulfillment in life, or to have others know them and to know themselves—will not be met. Believing in these role themes can lead to a shorter life span due to the stress created trying to fulfill these role requirements.

• The socialization of women often results in women seeing themselves and other women as less than men. This is not surprising given the themes of the messages they receive:

○ **You are valued for how you look.** Society views women as sex objects whose value decreases as they get older. The results of this theme can include eating disorders and plastic surgery. External accomplishments don't count and may actually detract from a woman's attractiveness.

○ **Be a cheerleader and stay on the sidelines.** Women are expected to admire and validate the male characteristics in men, but not to demonstrate these behaviors in themselves. Shows of competence on the part of women are taken as unexpected and out of the ordinary. As a result, women may fear demonstrating their own power or be uncomfortable with their position as an authority figure.

○ **Nurture others.** Be "other-directed" to a fault, always paying attention to what others need, especially men. Women should learn to be good listeners, empathic and good at performing service work and roles.

○ **Be passive and weak.** If women show their strength, they may be labeled as a bitch, a witch, or a "ball breaker." Women should be ladies—polite and nonassertive—which of course means they need protection by men. Tied into this theme is the idea that women are nothing without a man and are only valued through their attachments to a man as his wife, daughter, or mother.

- The bottom line is that society views women as inferior to men, which is often demonstrated in the workplace by pay inequity and the "glass ceiling."

- It is almost impossible not to have bought into these messages to some degree. If a women does manage to get out of these role prescripts, she is often treated in a violent or hostile way by men and even by other women. If a man goes against the male prescripts and tries to meet his psychological needs, he may be seen by the society as less manly, or he may consider himself to be a failure as a man.

Activity 2: Myths and Messages

1. Distribute the worksheets and ask if anyone has comments or questions about the themes it lists.

2. Form same-gender groups and have them discuss the worksheet using the following questions:

   ✔ Which of these themes are not healthy for you to believe in and act on (which are truly myths)?

   ✔ How have these themes caused problems or difficulties for you?

   ✔ What are the consequences of believing such messages?

   ✔ How could you rewrite each theme to become a healthy message for you and others of your gender?

   ☞ *Record these on an easel sheet.*

3. After about 30 minutes, reconvene the entire group and have participants share what they discussed and their new lists of healthier gender role message themes.

4. Ask for any closing insights or observations.

SOCIALIZATION THEMES

For Men

1. Do not be a sissy (feminine or girl-like).
   - Reject vulnerability.
   - Do not get close to other boys or men.

2. Be a big wheel.
   - Achieve wealth, fame, or success (external things).
   - Compete and show your superiority.
   - Select an attractive woman as a symbol of your success.

3. Be self-reliant and go it alone.
   - Show confidence and toughness.
   - Never ask for help.

4. Be a warrior in life.
   - Enjoy aggression, even violence.
   - Take risks.

For Women

1. You are valued for how you look.
   - Maintain youth and beauty. You are a sex object and will lose value as you age.
   - Don't strive for external accomplishments or personal fame or success.

2. Be the cheerleader (of men's accomplishments).
   - Do not act too competent.
   - Be on the periphery of life.
   - Attach yourself to a successful man.

3. Always nurture others.
   - Be other-directed to a fault.
   - Perform service jobs and tasks.

4. Be passive and weak.
   - Be a lady, polite and weak.
   - Believe that you're only valued for your attachments to men ("you're nothing without a man"), look for male protection.

25 GENDER QUIZ

In this fun, "game show" exercise, participants answer questions about gender behavior as they learn new information about communication between genders.

GOALS

To learn about typical patterns of male and female communication behavior.

To discuss gender socialization.

To have some fun.

GROUP SIZE

Unlimited.

TIME

$1^1/_2$ hours.

MATERIALS

Two buzzers or bells; a fun "prize" for half the group.

PROCESS

Activity 1: The Gender Quiz

1. Explain that this next exercise should be a fun way to learn facts and generalizations about gender behavior.

2. Form 2 mixed-gender groups including the same number of male and female participants and have each group sit in a circle across the room from the other.

3. Provide the following instructions:

   ➤ This exercise operates like a game show—a contest between the 2 groups.

   ➤ A member from each group will be sent to answer questions about their gender.

➤ Before "contestants" can answer a question, they must first ring the buzzer—the first person to "ring in" gets the first chance to answer the question.

➤ If they answer correctly, their group receives 10 points.

➤ If they answer incorrectly, their group loses 10 points and the contestant from the other group can answer the same question or pass.

➤ If the contestant from the second group answers the question correctly, their group receives 5 points; if they answer incorrectly, they lose 5 points.

➤ If they pass, their group neither gains nor loses any points.

➤ Groups must rotate contestants after every 2 questions.

➤ The group can help coach contestants, but the contestant has only 15 seconds to confer with his or her group.

➤ I will be the final judge of the answers. My answers are final and are based on extensive gender research in the fields of sociology, psychology, and linguistics.

➤ The group with the most points at the end of the contest receives a prize.

4. Ask if anyone has questions about the instructions.

5. Conduct the activity using the **Gender Quiz Questions** at the end of the exercise.

   ☞ *The questions are in no particular order. Some are more difficult than others, so you may want to save the more difficult ones for last. Make sure to always provide the correct answer and the explanatory information accompanying it.*

6. When you have run out of time or questions, present the prize(s) to the group with the most points.

Activity 2: Gender Quiz Results

1. Use the following comments to segue from the "fun" of the quiz to examining the serious issues they learned:

   • We have had some fun during the "Game Show," and at the same time you learned some generalizations in the field of gender studies.

   • Keep in mind these are generalizations and may not apply to any one specific person's behavior.

---

2. Form mixed-groups of 6–8 participants and have them discuss the following questions:

✔ What new information did you gain?

✔ How can these new insights be helpful to you, especially in the workplace?

✔ What can you do to challenge yourself to move out of stereotypical gender role behavior?

3. Reconvene the entire group and invite participants to share their insights.

4. End by encouraging participants to pay attention to and discuss any gender patterns they notice as the group continues to work together.

VARIATIONS

■ Develop questions of your own that are relevant to your organization.

■ Present a chalktalk on gender role behavior or invite someone from a local college to speak on the topic.

Gender Quiz Questions

1. **Which gender tells jokes the most?** [Men—also, male humor tends to be more hostile and acts as a bonding technique for men.]

2. **75–90% of conversational interruptions come from which gender?** [Men—men will even answer questions not addressed to them. Women tend to wait for pauses to talk and their comments are often interrupted, overlooked, or not heard.]

3. **During a conversation, who is more likely to give support and approval and how do they do it?** [Women—they nod their heads, say things like "uh-uh," "interesting," or "tell me more."]

4. **Who talks the most in conversations?** [Men]

5. **Which is the most intuitive gender?** [Neither–however, women pay greater attention to detail and pay more attention to nonverbal communication, which could make them "appear" more intuitive.]

6. **Who is the most friendly in an initial meeting and how do they tend to display this friendliness?** [Women—through nonverbal communication such as smiling and making eye contact]

©1995 Whole Person Press 210 W Michigan Duluth MN 55802   (800) 247-6789

7. **Why do men tend to want some time alone when they come home from work?** [All day they have used language as a way to negotiate status and want to be free not to talk at home. Women feel they have to be careful at work about what and how they say things, so at home they need to share what has happened during their day.]

8. **How do women and men tend to respond to someone sharing a problem with them?** [Women tend to use active listening, sharing the feelings they hear; men tend to propose solutions to the problems.]

9. **Which gender tends to be more self-critical and apologetic?** [Women]

10. **Which gender is more emotional when they talk?** [Neither—women use the phrase "I feel" and show tears more often; men get louder and show anger through yelling and swearing.]

11. **When conversing, which gender brings up the most topics?** [Women]

12. **Which gender is more likely to bring up problems and confront issues?** [Women]

13. **Which group of women enjoys better mental health—those who work both inside and outside the home or those who spend all their time at home with their children?** [Those who work both inside and outside the home]

14. **Why was the word "sex" added to title vii of the Civil Rights Act of 1964?** [It was added as a joke in an attempt to get the bill defeated.]

15. **Who invented the cotton gin?** [Catherine Greene, but since women could not be inventors at that time, Eli Whitney built the machine for her and got the credit.]

16. **Which gender's suicide rate doubles after divorce?** [Men's]

17. **Which gender's economic status declines as much as fifty percent after divorce?** [Women's]

18. **Of the Fortune 500 and Service 500 companies, women make up less than what percent of senior managers (those at or above the level of vice-president)?** [Five percent, according to a 1990 survey]

19. **What is the main reason men communicate?** [To maintain status]

20. **What is the main reason women communicate?** [To create connections with others]

©1995 Whole Person Press 210 W Michigan Duluth MN 55802   (800) 247-6789

21. **In school, teachers tend to call on which gender the most?** [Boys, even when they don't have their hands up, often ignoring girls who have their hands raised. Both male and female teachers exhibit this trait.]

22. **During a discussion, which gender is most likely to disagree with or ignore others?** [Men]

23. **True or false: according to a recent study, the more capable a woman is at performing a task, the more likely she is to be treated positively?** [False]

©1995 Whole Person Press 210 W Michigan Duluth MN 55802   (800) 247-6789

26 SEXISM

Using worksheet examples, male participants share and discuss their sexism and women participants their internalized sexism.

GOALS

To better understand sexism and internalized sexism.

To examine how sexism and internalized sexism operates in ourselves.

To explore the impact of and ways to eliminate sexist and internalized sexist behavior in the workplace.

GROUP SIZE

Unlimited (but requires one facilitator for every 8–10 participants).

TIME

2–2$\frac{1}{2}$ hours.

MATERIALS

Easels and easel paper; magic markers; masking tape; **Internalized Sexism** worksheet; **Sexism** worksheet.

PROCESS

☞ *This exercise works best if conducted after either Exercises 7, 23, or 24, the socialization messages exercises.*

Activity 1: Sexism and Internalized Sexism Chalktalk

1. Define internalized sexism:
   - Internalized sexism occurs when women buy into negative messages about women, especially those that say that women are inferior to or less valuable than men.
   - It also occurs when women participate in their own oppression and can be very painful for women to examine in themselves.
   - Internalized sexism has been a major factor preventing women from realizing and putting into action their intelligence and power; in other words, it causes women to limit themselves.

©1995 Whole Person Press 210 W Michigan Duluth MN 55802   (800) 247-6789

- It often makes relationships between women stressful.
- Women are not always aware of their own internalized sexism.

2. Distribute the **Internalized Sexism** worksheet and highlight some specific examples that pertain to the workplace.

3. Define sexism:

   - Sexism occurs when men believe—at least on some level—that they are superior to women, and having the power, society reinforces that belief.

   - Sexism can range from ignoring women to committing abusive and violent acts toward them.

   - Sexism, or power over women, gives men concrete benefits and privileges they find hard to give up.

   - Men are often unaware of their own sexism, which only helps to perpetuate gender-based inequities.

     ☞ *It is often hard for men to understand the concept that they have privilege simply because they are men; the mechanisms that give men privilege are often invisible to men. Whereas women so often experience marginality in their lives, they are aware of not having gender privileges. Racial, social, and heterosexual privileges also play a role in our social development and should also be covered at some point.*

   - Sexism also oppresses men: while they may have power over women they usually do not have a great deal of power over their own lives.

4. Distribute the **Sexism** worksheets and highlight some of the key examples, presenting specific examples that pertain to the workplace.

Activity 2: Worksheets

1. Divide participants into mixed-gender groups of 7–9 participants and move the groups to separate meeting areas.

2. Instruct them to spend 5 minutes filling out their worksheets; the men should check off the items on the **Sexism** worksheet that fit their behavior or attitudes and the women should check off the items on the **Internalized Sexism** sheet that fit their behavior or attitudes.

3. When they have finished allow each individual to share their list, giving specific examples that pertain to each checked item and discussing the items with the group.

☞ *Do not get stuck too long on any one item, such as opening doors (often used by men as a way to justify sexism; point out that if opening doors and other similar behavior is respectful of women, then men also deserve the same respect).*

4. After about 90 minutes, reconvene the entire group and ask participants to share any insights they may have gained during the exercise.

5. End the exercise by thanking participants for their openness.

©1995 Whole Person Press 210 W Michigan Duluth MN 55802   (800) 247-6789

INTERNALIZED SEXISM

❑ Finding fault and harshly criticizing other women, including women leaders

❑ Insulting women leaders

❑ Mistrusting other women

❑ Protecting men and validating their masculinity

❑ Adapting behavior to be like some men, such as laughing at and telling sex/gender jokes

❑ Calling women "girls"

❑ Believing that women are not as good as men

❑ Not sharing one's opinions, ideas, or beliefs

❑ Seeing oneself as the exception: "I'm not like other women"

❑ Valuing men's opinions more than women's and believing that a man's approval is worth more than a woman's

❑ Not supporting other women or not networking with women

❑ Believing the negative messages about women

❑ Allowing men to verbally or physically abuse you

❑ Trying to become like men in behavior, speech, dress, manners, interests, etc.

❑ Being embarrassed by another woman's behavior, believing she is "giving women a bad name"

❑ Putting men first

❑ Questioning or blaming oneself

❑ Settling for less than you want

❑ Avoiding leadership and authority positions

❑ Acting the perpetual "girl"

❑ Always being nice and polite and not confronting issues directly

©1995 Whole Person Press 210 W Michigan Duluth MN 55802   (800) 247-6789

SEXISM

❑ Dominating discussions and/or ignoring women

❑ Attributing contributions made by a woman to a man or restating what a woman has just said

❑ Telling and laughing at gender/sex jokes (even when only men are present)

❑ Assuming women cannot do a job or cannot do it as well as men

❑ Believing women are hired and promoted because of affirmative action and not because they are qualified

❑ Calling women "girls," "honey," "sweetheart," etc.

❑ Keeping some information about the job or organization from women

❑ Considering certain behaviors when exhibited by men as positive and when exhibited by women as negative

❑ Using words or phrases to make women feel out of place or talking crudely about women

❑ Being condescending and paternalistic to women

❑ Giving and assigning women to "helping" roles

❑ Not accepting a woman's authority on the job

❑ Engaging in activities that exclude women from informal networks

❑ Attributing one woman's behavior to all women

❑ Believing that men are superior to women

❑ Protecting women—apologizing only to women for crude language in a mixed-gender group, opening doors only for women, standing up when only women enter a room

❑ Competing with men and taking their ideas seriously while expecting only polite attention and support from women

❑ _____

❑ _____

27 HOMOPHOBIA AND SEXISM

By dispelling myths with facts, this exercise examines homophobia, its parallels to sexism, and its effect on the workplace.

GOALS

To examine homophobia and heterosexism in the workplace.

To explore the parallels between homophobia and sexism.

To dispel myths about sexual orientation.

To heighten awareness of the effect homophobia has on the workplace.

GROUP SIZE

10–30 participants.

TIME

2–3 hours.

MATERIALS

Easel and easel paper; magic markers; masking tape.

PROCESS

Activity 1: Early Experiences

1. Introduce the topic with the following chalktalk:

   - Homophobia is the irrational fear and hatred of gays, lesbians, and bisexuals. It exists in most organizations today and in our society at large.

   - Gays, lesbians, and bisexuals have been the invisible minority in organizations, and many are now coming "out of the closet" to demand their equal rights.

   - Homophobia helps to keep all people in rigid, gender-based roles that inhibit self-expression:

     ○ The fear of being considered gay keeps men from being intimate with their male friends.

     ○ The same fear locks us into rigid definitions of masculinity and femininity, affecting our working and personal relationships.

- As children, we were taught clear messages about deviating from heterosexuality—even before we fully understood relationships, intimacy, and sexuality.

2. Ask each participant to respond to the following questions:

✔ As a child, what names did you hear people call gays, lesbians, and bisexuals?

☞ *List these labels on the easel chart.*

✔ What stereotypes did people associate with gays, lesbians, and bisexuals?

✔ What personal experiences have you had with lesbians, gays, and bisexuals?

☞ *These questions help to identify the myths most of us have been taught about homosexuality and encourage participants to share their feelings in a nonjudgmental atmosphere. Lesbians, gays, and bisexuals in the group may or may not identify themselves.*

3. Lead a discussion of what their answers revealed about what they have learned about sexual orientation.

☞ *Note that many of the negative terms used as labels for gays and lesbians are also used to keep men and women in line and to encourage certain types of male and female behavior, defining society's limits on acceptable masculinity and femininity.*

Activity 2: Myths and Facts

1. Form mixed gender groups of 8–10 participants, assign a facilitator to each, and provide the following instructions:

☞ *If your group has gays, lesbians, or bisexuals who are "out," do not put them all in the same group—split them up to give more diversity to each group.*

➤ Identify the myths—or what you think are myths—you have learned about homosexuality.

➤ Your facilitator will record each of these on a separate easel sheet.

➤ You have 20 minutes to think of as many myths as you can.

2. After 20 minutes, ask the groups to report their lists using the procedure below:

➤ One group reads a myth and posts it on the wall.

> Other groups with a similar myth post it in the same area.

> The next group reads one of their myths, posts it on the wall, and other groups post similar myths with it.

> Continue the process until all the myths have been posted.

3. Then take each major myth and use the **Homosexuality Myths and Facts** list to lead a discussion about the facts that contradict the myth.

☞ *Include additional information and invite any "out" lesbians, gays, or bisexuals to share information.*

Activity 3: Speak Out

1. Ask "out" homosexual and bisexual participants to talk about their personal experiences.

   ☞ *Participants who are open about their sexual orientation and willing to share can do more than anything else to help personalize the issues. Talk to them ahead of time about your expectations and get their permission to discuss their lives.*

2. After each person has shared what they want to about their life as a gay man, lesbian, or bisexual, ask the other participants if they have any questions for the speakers.

3. Conclude by asking the gays, lesbians, and bisexuals to share with the group what they would like from heterosexual people—for instance, how they would like their allies to support them and what they never want people to say or do.

4. Reform the small groups and have participants share what they learned and how they can apply these lessons in the workplace.

VARIATIONS

■ If you do not have anyone in the group who is out of the closet and willing to talk about their personal experiences, arrange for several people to come to the group to talk about being gay, lesbian or bisexual.

■ If you have a group that would like to know more about the history of homosexuality, show **Before Stonewall**, an excellent video available at most book and video stores. Another video resource is **One Nation Under God**, a PBS video available at some select video stores.

Homosexuality Myths and Facts

1. **Myth:** I don't know any gay, lesbian, or bisexual people.

   Fact: Since a significant percentage of the population is gay, lesbian, or bisexual (perhaps 10 percent), you do know these people, though they may not be open about their sexual orientation. They are doctors, lawyers, members of the clergy, politicians, your coworkers, athletes, teachers, business people, etc.

2. **Myth:** Homosexuality is a choice and people could change if they wanted to.

   Fact: The majority of research studies indicate that some people may change their behavior because pressure from the heterosexual society is so great. However, they do not change their underlying desire or orientation.

3. **Myth:** It is abnormal and sick to be lesbian, gay, or bisexual.

   Fact: The American Psychological Association says that homosexuality is not an illness. (It is homophobia that needs to be cured).

4. **Myth:** Homosexuality is immoral or a sin.

   Fact: Although some religious organization preach this, many other religious denominations do not. (Most religions teach that hatred and intolerance is wrong).

5. **Myth:** Lesbians, gays, and bisexuals do not make good parents (or teachers) and will raise their children (or recruit their students to their sexual orientation.).

   Fact: Many gays, bisexuals, and lesbians have been married and have children or have adopted children. Studies find they are no more or less loving or caring than heterosexuals. A recent study showed that gay parents do not raise gay children. Sexual orientation is not something you can catch or teach.

6. **Myth:** Gay men are child molesters.

   Fact: The majority of child molesters and abusers are heterosexual and/or pedophiles. (A pedophile is an adult who seeks sex with children and generally does not have sexual relationships with other adults; many have sex with children of both genders.) Heterosexual rape is much more common than homosexual rape of either adults or children.

©1995 Whole Person Press 210 W Michigan Duluth MN 55802   (800) 247-6789

7. **Myth:** You can tell gays or lesbians from their appearance or behavior.

   Fact: Gays and lesbians have not been found to be similar to the other gender in their psychological functioning. There is as much variety in the look and behavior of gays and lesbians as there is among heterosexuals.

8. **Myth:** Gays, lesbians, and bisexuals are promiscuous and do not maintain long-term relationships.

   Fact: Gays, lesbians, and bisexuals form a variety of relationships—including marriage—just like heterosexuals.

9. **Myth:** AIDS is a gay disease.

   Fact: It is true that in this country the majority of those infected with HIV are gay males, but that is not true in other countries. More and more heterosexuals in the United States have become infected with HIV.

10. **Myth:** Gays and lesbians will corrupt their colleagues if homosexuality is legalized.

    Fact: Gays and lesbians are not interested in sexual relationships with unwilling heterosexual colleagues.

28 IF I WOKE UP TOMORROW AS

In an effort to better understand their colleagues, participants imagine how their lives would change if they woke up the next day as the other gender.

GOALS

To better understand the other gender.

To better understand how society views each gender and the effect that has on self-esteem and life choices.

GROUP SIZE

Unlimited.

TIME

2 hours.

MATERIALS

Pens and pencils; **Gender Experiences** worksheets.

PROCESS

Activity 1: Who Do You Admire?

1. Ask participants to silently consider the following:

    ☞ *Give them a few minutes to think through each task before moving on to the next task.*

    ➤ Think of a man you admire and consider which of his characteristics have won your admiration.

    ➤ Now think of that same man as if he were a woman with the same characteristics. Would you admire her just the same? Why or why not?

    ➤ Next think of a woman you admire and consider which of her characteristics have won your admiration.

    ➤ Now think of that same woman as if she were a man with the same characteristics. Would you admire him just the same? Why or why not?

2. Have participants form pairs and discuss what they thought about during *Step 1*.

3. After about 10 minutes, reconvene the entire group and have them share any insights they gained through the activity.

Activity 2: Reverse Experience

1. Introduce Activity 2 with the following points:

   • In the first activity, you began to think about how society views each gender and the differences in those views.

   • Imagine you woke up tomorrow morning and found that you were the other gender. How would you and your life be the same? How would it be different?

   • Let's find out.

2. Distribute the **Gender Experiences** worksheets and provide the following instructions:

   ➤ The worksheet contains a number of items pertaining to different aspects of your life.

   ➤ Decide whether each item would remain the same or change if you woke up tomorrow as the other gender and check the appropriate box.

   ➤ Then explain why you checked "Same" or "Different" by writing a few comments in the space under "Explain." Begin.

3. Call time after 10 minutes and form mixed-gender groups of 6–8 participants and have them use the following questions to discuss their responses:

   ✔ Which aspects of your life would remain the same?

   ✔ Which would be different?

   ✔ What items would cause major changes in your life?

   ✔ Did any items surprise, upset, or excite you?

   ✔ What questions or issues does this raise for you?

   ✔ What did you learn from this activity?

4. Reconvene the entire group and have each small group share their insights.

©1995 Whole Person Press 210 W Michigan Duluth MN 55802   (800) 247-6789

GENDER EXPERIENCES

	Same	Diff.	Explain
1. Your job or career			
2. Available role models & mentors at work			
3. The overall treatment you receive at work			
4. Media images of your gender			
5. Your gender's role in your religion			
6. The treatment you receive in commercial establishments			
7. The colleagues you socialize with and where you meet			
8. Your expected level of responsibility to household tasks			
9. Where you go on vacations if single			
10. The treatment you would receive in bars or night clubs			
11. Your relationships with and care for children			

GENDER EXPERIENCES, continued

	Same	Diff.	Explain
12. Your credibility in presentations and meetings			
13. Possibility of career advancement			
14. The amount of time you would spend on your appearance			
15. The way others respond to your body			
16. The treatment you receive in public spaces			
17. How you feel and think about sex			
18. How society views you			
19. Risks of physical and sexual assault			
20. Your privileges/level of power			
21. Your relationships with the other gender			
22. Your relationships with the same gender			

©1995 Whole Person Press 210 W Michigan Duluth MN 55802   (800) 247-6789

29 LEADING AND FOLLOWING

Men lead women and women lead men in order to explore how genders respond to and interact with one another in supervisory and subordinate roles.

GOALS

To experience how it feels to lead and to follow.

To become aware of how both men and women respond to leaders of the other gender.

To understand which role—leader or follower—participants are most comfortable with.

GROUP SIZE

Unlimited.

TIME

$1^1/_2$ hours.

MATERIALS

Easels and easel paper; magic markers; masking tape.

PROCESS

Activity 1: Women Lead; Men Lead

1. Briefly describe the exercise and its goals before providing the following instructions:

   ➤ Men, go to one end of the room; women to the opposite end.

   ➤ The women will start as leaders. Decide what you want a man to do for or with you and then approach a man and try to get him to perform the task.

   ➤ The men should respond honestly—you may choose to perform the task or resist.

   ➤ After 5 minutes, we will reverse the roles.

   ➤ Try to be aware of what you are feeling in each role. Begin.

©1995 Whole Person Press 210 W Michigan Duluth MN 55802   (800) 247-6789

2. After 5 minutes, call time and allow participants to express their feelings by asking them to discuss how they chose to lead or respond and what reactions each partner had to the others actions.

3. Repeat *Step 1* , providing these instructions:

   ➤ The men should choose a different woman from the partner they were just with.

   ➤ Remember, each man should approach a woman and try to get her to do something with or for him. The women should respond honestly and can either perform the task or resist.

4. After 5 minutes, call time and repeat *Step 2*.

Activity 2: Gender Socialization

1. Form same-gender groups of 6–8 participants and have them list on one easel sheet the feelings they had while leading and on another easel sheet the feelings they had while following.

2. When their lists are complete, have them discuss the first activity using the following questions:

   ✔ Were you more comfortable leading or following? What contributed to this feeling? Is this the way you normally respond?

   ✔ How have you been socialized as a woman or man regarding leading and following? What messages have you received about women leading? about men leading? about women following? about men following?

   ✔ What leadership style did you use—how did you try to get your partner to follow? Is this a typical style your gender uses in the workplace?

   ✔ What style of leadership do you prefer from women?

   ✔ What style of leadership do you prefer from men?

   ✔ Were there any moments when you resented your partner? When did you feel this and why? How did you handle your feelings?

   ✔ Would you like to follow more? What would you have to give up? What would you gain?

   ✔ Would you like to lead more? What would you have to give up? What would you gain?

   ✔ What have you learned about your reactions to the other gender as leaders? Is there anything you think you might want to explore or work on further?

3. Reconvene the entire group, ask the men to move to the center of the room and form a circle, and give them 15 minutes to read their easel lists and discuss any significant insights they have gained.

   ☞ *Allow questions from either group and encourage any additional insights.*

4. Repeat *Step 3* with the women in the center.

5. End by asking participants to share what they learned they need to work on regarding their responses to and behavior around the leadership approaches of different genders.

VARIATIONS

■ Instead of or in addition to Activity 1, have each gender group design an activity in which they lead the other.

■ Form smaller mixed-gender groups and have each participant lead a group of the opposite gender.

©1995 Whole Person Press 210 W Michigan Duluth MN 55802   (800) 247-6789

30 LANGUAGE

Participants explore the effect language has on gender attitudes and self image and learn how to eliminate gender bias in communications.

GOALS

To become aware of how language affects gender attitudes.

To understand the role language plays in self-image.

To explore using nonsexist language.

GROUP SIZE

20–30 participants.

TIME

$1^1/_2$ hours.

MATERIALS

Easels and easel paper; magic markers; masking tape; **For Men Only** worksheets; **For Women Only** worksheets.

PROCESS

Activity 1: Ice Breaker

1. Begin the session by asking gender groups to brainstorm separate lists of terms:

   ➤ Men, brainstorm words that represent some of the worst things a man can be called.

   ☞ *Record these words on an easel chart. They may include terms such as wimp, sissy, faggot, girl, homo, etc.*

   ➤ Women, brainstorm words that represent some of the worst things a woman can be called.

   ☞ *Record these words on an easel chart. They may include terms such as slut, cunt, whore, bitch, etc.*

2. Use the questions below to discuss the lists they created:

   ✔ What did you notice about the list for women? about the list for men?

©1995 Whole Person Press 210 W Michigan Duluth MN 55802   (800) 247-6789

✔ What implications do these words have as far as sending behavioral messages to men and women?

✔ When you were growing up, did anyone ever use any of these words to refer to you or other members of your gender? What impact did that have on you?

✔ Do you ever use these words? In what context? How do you feel about using these words?

3. Thank them for their honesty and explain that the next activity explores the impact language has on our self esteem and gender images.

Activity 2: The Impact of Language

1. Distribute the **For Men Only** worksheets to the men and the **For Women Only** worksheets to the women and allow 5 minutes to fill them out.

   ☞ *Encourage participants to be honest in their responses. At this point do not give each person copies of the other gender's handout. Tell them they may see it later.*

2. After 5 minutes, distribute the **For Men Only** worksheets to the women and ask the men to move to the center of the room.

3. Have the male facilitators use the questions below to lead the men in a discussion of their responses as the women listen in:

   ✔ How would you feel if you grew up hearing the terms on this list and if they were used in our everyday language?

   ✔ How would you react to being referred to by the specific terms? How would that impact you?

   ✔ Can you think of additional terms currently used in reference to women that would bother you?

   ✔ If society regularly used the terms on the worksheet, how would this affect you and other men?

   ✔ In what ways does sexist language perpetuate stereotypes?

4. Thank the men for their honesty and give them each a copy of the **For Women Only** worksheets.

5. Ask the women to move to the center of the room and have the female facilitators use the questions below to lead the women in a discussion of their responses as the men listen in:

©1995 Whole Person Press 210 W Michigan Duluth MN 55802   (800) 247-6789

✔ How, in general, did you react to the terms? What impact have they had on your thinking about women, men, and yourself?

✔ How did you react to the specific terms? Which ones really annoy you? Are there any others you would add?

✔ Have you ever complained about any of these terms? Why or why not? If you did say you found some language offensive, what response did you get?

✔ If you were a man, how do you think the terms would impact how you thought about men and women?

✔ What impact does sexist language have on your self-image? Give an example if you can.

6. Reconvene the entire group and allow time for individuals to ask questions regarding either gender.

7. Conclude by making several points about the impact of sexist language:

- Some women may feel invisible, less than men, or not included when they are subsumed under a supposedly universal male term (i.e., "fireman" instead of "fire fighter").

- If women complain about language they are often made to feel that they are nitpicking or making a big deal out of nothing.

- Men generally do not notice or think about the impact words may have on their thinking and behavior.

- Many women also have not noticed the influence language has on them and other women and have accepted sexist language.

- Consider these other issues involved with sexist language when you speak:

  ○ When a speaker attaches a gender modifier to occupations (lady doctor, the cleaning guy) it often implies that the gender mentioned does not normally or should not hold that position.

  ○ Using "girl" or "boy" when referring to an adult is condescending and implies dependency associated with children.

  ○ Use of "my" as in "my assistant" may indicate that the speaker thinks of the assistant as personal property. Avoid this by using their name or title: "I'll ask the administrative assistant."

  ○ It is patronizing and unnecessary to use the adjective "little" as in "a terrific little worker" when describing a fellow employee.

  ○ It is unnecessary to refer to or emphasize anyone's marital status.

- Hopefully this exercise has given all of us some insight.

Activity 3: Nonsexist Language

1. Form mixed-gender groups of 4–6 participants and assign them the following task:

   ➤ Develop some nonsexist terms.

   ➤ Choose someone to record them on a sheet of easel paper.

   ☞ For example, "humans" instead of "mankind", "right person for the job" instead of "right man for the job," "members of Congress" instead of "congressmen," "sales representative" instead of "salesman," etc.

2. After 30 minutes reconvene the entire group and have each small group read their lists.

3. Use their examples to expand on the following points:

   - Use parallel words when specifying gender, such as "men and women," not "men and ladies."

   - Address both female and male perspectives with terms like "employees" and "spouses."

   - Use gender-neutral words or phrases in your language, such as "journalist" and "fire fighter."

   - When referring to both genders, make sure to use gender-neutral pronouns.

   - Avoid describing men by their profession and women by their appearance.

   - Be respectful of both genders and don't stereotype.

4. Discuss how they can help each other use bias-free language and what possible reactions they may get from others.

FOR MEN ONLY

Directions: Imagine that society in general uses the following terms and phrases which are meant to include men or refer to men. Indicate which ones you find acceptable (A) or unacceptable (U) and briefly explain why.

General Terms	A	U	Explain
1. Womankind (meant to include all people)			
2. Herstory (books and classes about nations, people)			
3. Herstory of Woman (includes history of all)			
4. God portrayed as a woman and referred to as "She."			
5. Woman (for "all women and men")			
6. Gals (meant to include men and women)			
7. Year of the Man			
8. Best woman for the job			
9. Workwoman's compensation			
10. The weaker sex (referring to men)			

FOR MEN ONLY, continued

Specific terms referring to men	A	U	Explain
11. He is the chair-woman of the task force			
12. Congresswoman			
13. Mr. Susan James (being identified by your spouse's name)			
14. Mistress of Arts or Science Degree			
15. Gentleman lawyer, doctor, etc.			
16. The little gentleman			
17. My old gentleman			
18. He's a sissy boy			
19. Terrific little salesman			
20. My boy will call your boy			

©1995 Whole Person Press 210 W Michigan Duluth MN 55802   (800) 247-6789

FOR WOMEN ONLY

Directions: The following are words and phrases often used in our society to include women or refer to women. Indicate whether you find them acceptable (A) or unacceptable (U) and briefly explain why.

Specific Terms	A	U	Explain
1. Mankind			
2. History (books and classes about nations, people)			
3. History of Man (includes history of all)			
4. God portrayed as a man and referred to as "He."			
5. Man (for "all women and men")			
6. Guys (meant to include men and women)			
7. Year of the Woman			
8. Right man for the job			
9. Workman's compensation			
10. The weaker sex (referring to women)			

FOR WOMEN ONLY, continued

Specific terms referring to women	A	U	Explain
11. Chairman			
12. Congressman			
13. Mrs. John James (being identified by your spouse's name)			
14. Master of Arts or Science Degree			
15. Lady lawyer, doctor, etc.			
16. Little lady			
17. My old lady			
18. She's a tomboy			
19. Terrific little saleswoman			
20. My girl will call your girl			

31 DOUBLE STANDARDS

Participants explore how certain work behavior is sometimes viewed differently depending on whether a man or woman exhibited the behavior. Makes a great follow-up exercise to Exercise 30.

GOALS

To identify the various assumptions we make while observing female and male behavior.

To understand how we interpret similar behaviors differently depending on which gender exhibits the behavior.

GROUP SIZE

Unlimited (but requires a facilitator for every group of 6–8 participants).

TIME

$1\frac{1}{2}$ hours.

MATERIALS

Easels and easel paper; magic markers; masking tape.

PROCESS

Activity 1: Double Standards in the Workplace

1. Introduce the exercise with the following comments:
   - In previous exercises we have gained insights as to the ways our patriarchal society views women and men.
   - In this exercise we continue to explore these ideas by examining assumptions we make about the behavior of men and women.

2. Form mixed gender groups of 6–8 participants, assign a facilitator to each group, and move them to separate spaces in the room (or to separate rooms).

3. Have each facilitator present the following task to her or his group:
   - ➤ Each time I name a behavior, you will identify what most people would normally say if they saw a man engaged in the activity and

what they would say if they saw a woman engaged in the same activity.

➤ We will record your responses on the easel chart.

4. Present five behaviors and record their responses following the format of the **"Double Standards" sample easel chart**.

    ☞ *Have facilitators use the sample chart for examples to start with, choosing three or four of the behaviors to work with. Do not tell them how a particular behavior might be interpreted. However, if a group is having difficulty understanding the task, have facilitator present one full example to get them started.*

5. Have each group develop five of their own workplace scenarios and record them following the format of the **"Double Standards" sample easel chart**.

6. After about 30 minutes, reconvene the entire group and have each group post their sheets on the wall and report the results of their work.

7. Ask participants how it feels to see that we often measure men and women with a different yardstick.

Activity 2: Action Plans

1. Form mixed-gender pairs and ask them to discuss the following questions:

    ☞ *Write the questions on an easel for all to see.*

    ✔ Which of the assumptions or interpretations you generated in the small groups have you made about the men and women you work with?

    ✔ Which ones would you like to change?

    ✔ We have demonstrated that even when women perform the same action as men they may be perceived as less capable or credible. What could you do in your workplace to change or prevent this from happening?

2. Reconvene the entire group and invite participants to share what they intend to work on.

"Double Standards" sample easel chart

Behavior	Men	Women
Talking in the hallway with a same-gender coworker	They're discussing a business deal.	They're gossiping.
Family picture on the desk	He's a responsible family man.	Family will come before her career.
Having lunch with the male boss	They're discussing his career or a business deal.	They're having an affair.
Going on a business trip	It's good for his career.	Is it okay with her husband?
Not in their office	He must be in a meeting.	She must be in the ladies' room.
Leaving the company	He's moving on to better things.	You can't depend on a woman.
Engaged to be married	He's settling down.	She'll get pregnant and leave.
Asking for a job to be done right	He's a great leader who I respect and look up to.	She's difficult and impossible, too demanding.

©1995 Whole Person Press 210 W Michigan Duluth MN 55802   (800) 247-6789

32 GROUP GENDER DYNAMICS

Participants develop a vision of a gender-bias free world and observe the gender dynamics of a work group.

GOALS

To become aware of gender-linked behaviors that affect performance in work teams.

To improve observation of gender-linked behaviors.

To visualize a gender-bias free world.

GROUP SIZE

Unlimited (but requires a facilitator for each group of 10–12 participants).

TIME

$2^1/_2$ hours.

MATERIALS

Easels and easel paper; magic markers; masking tape; **Observer Guide** worksheets.

PROCESS

Activity 1: Observations

1. Form mixed-gender groups of about 10–12 participants and ask 2 members of each group to leave the room with another facilitator for "special instructions."

    ☞ *The group members leaving the room will act as observers. Do not share the goals of the exercise with the participants who remain in the room. They should not know that their gender dynamics are being observed, as this could interfere with their natural behavior.*

2. Have the facilitator with the observers distribute and review the **Observer Guide** worksheets, providing the following instructions:

    ☞ *If you do not have many participants, have facilitators observe.*

➤ You are going to observe your group's gender dynamics as they work to create a vision of a gender-bias free world.

➤ Check behaviors you see participants engage in and make a few notes about what was said or done so you can be specific when giving feedback to your group.

➤ Make notes about observations on the second page, describing briefly what you see and if the behavior changes.

3. While the observers are receive their instructions, give the groups the following task:

➤ Describe what the world would be like without gender bias or prescribed gender roles.

➤ Record the elements of such a world on an easel sheet.

➤ You have 30 minutes.

➤ The members of your groups that left will return, sit outside your group and make notes on your progress.

4. Move the groups to separate spaces, have the observers join their groups, and tell them to begin.

☞ *A facilitator should also observe each group in order to better lead the feedback activity.*

5. Call time after 30 minutes, reconvene the entire group, and have each group read their vision.

6. Give the group members a short break so you can meet the observers and make a chart of their observations.

☞ *Follow the format of the **Observer Guide** worksheet. Prepare the chart ahead of time on an easel sheet and fill in the numbers based on the sum of each observer's sheet.*

Activity 2: Gender Dynamics Feedback

1. Reconvene the entire group and explain that:

• Not only was your progress being monitored, but the observers also noted your group's gender dynamics.

• You will now have an opportunity to explore what those dynamics involved and how they affected your performance.

2. Distribute copies of the **Observer Guide** worksheets and explain that the observers used the guide to monitor the groups.

3. Invite one of the small groups to sit in the middle of the room ask them to discuss what gender dynamics they noticed while they performed the task.

4. Then ask the group's observers to share their observations.

   ☞ *Add any observations you or another facilitator made.*

5. Select another group and repeat *Steps 3* and *4* until each group has had a turn.

6. Reveal the chart of the total numbers regarding the gender dynamics and go over the information.

7. Lead a discussion about the group's prevalent gender-role and equal-role behaviors.

8. Form same-gender groups and have them discuss what they learned, which mixed-gender group behaviors they would like to change, and those mixed-gender group behaviors they consider positive.

VARIATIONS

■ Instead of an entire group feedback session, change Activity 2 so participants remain in their task groups.

OBSERVER GUIDE

Activity	Male	Female	What was said/done and by whom
1. Number of times talked			
2. Used short phrases			
3. Used long statements			
4. Became detached and distanced self from the group			
5. Used apologetic phrases or deferred to others			
6. Interrupted others			
7. Initiated ideas, made suggestions, shared thoughts			
8. Shared feelings			
9. Used questions, inquiring & qualifying statements			
10. Made confronting statements, found fault			
11. Used supportive statements, added a thought			

OBSERVER GUIDE , continued

Activity	Male	Female	What was said/done and by whom
12. Used active listening responses			
13. Used nonverbal support			
14. Initiated touch			
15. Told joke(s)			
16. Made sexual or sexist remarks			
17. Stressed task completion			
18. Used patronizing remarks			

Physical Set Up (Are women and men segregated? Does any gender occupy a dominant or power position, such as at the easel or head of the table? Does anyone try to control the group by standing up or by taking up extra space?)

Gender Assumptions (Is either gender over- or under-challenged? Is a woman assigned note taking? Is a man in the leadership role?)

Write other gender observations on the back

33 LEADERSHIP STYLES

Designed for managers and supervisors, this exercise helps participants understand typical male and female leadership styles as well as their own and those of their colleagues.

GOALS

To understand what leadership traits or characteristics each gender has been socialized to develop and exhibit.

To explore which leadership traits the group's organization values.

To expand the definition of successful and effective management.

GROUP SIZE

Unlimited.

TIME

$2^1/_2$ hours.

MATERIALS

Easels and easel paper; magic markers; masking tape; **Typical Leadership Styles** worksheets.

PROCESS

Activity 1: The Ideal Manager

☞ *Do not share the title of this session or its goals at this point—it may affect the participants' performance.*

1. Form small mixed-gender groups of 6-8 participants, assign a facilitator to each group, and move them to separate meeting spaces.

2. Have the groups create a composite of the ideal manager's qualities and record it on an easel chart—they do not have to reach a consensus, although they should discuss the items before recording them.

   ☞ *While they are working in their groups, each facilitator should list participants' names across the top of a sheet of easel paper.*

3. When they have finished, place the facilitators' chart next to the groups' list and draw lines underneath each trait, across both charts.

4. Under their names, have participants check off the traits they consider their strengths.

5. When all have finished, use the following questions to help participants find gender-related patterns:

   ✔ Which traits do more men possess? more women? What might this mean?

   ✔ Do any of the traits correspond with those your organization says it is looking for now? Does the company ever fail to promote employees that have those traits? What gender, if either, tends to exhibit these traits?

   ✔ What leadership characteristics have women been socialized to develop? men?

   ✔ Does anyone in the group tend to exhibit traits that have traditionally been identified with the other gender? If so, has that helped or hindered the person to grow within their organization?

Activity 2: Ways Women Lead; Ways Men Lead

1. Reconvene the entire group and introduce the next activity by making the following points:

   • In a minute you are going to get a worksheet containing the results of some recent research on gender leadership by Dr. Judy Rosener, a faculty member at the Graduate School of Management at the University of California.

   • This research has led to some generalizations about male and female leadership styles.

   • Remember, these are only generalizations and may not fit any individuals here.

2. Distribute the worksheets and give participants about 10 minutes to fill them out.

3. After 10 minutes, have participants rejoin their small groups and use the following questions to discuss what they learned or discovered as they completed the worksheets:

   ✔ What are the advantages and disadvantages of male and female leadership styles in light of most organizations' changing cultures?

   ✔ Did you learn to take on many of the characteristics associated with your gender's leadership style? If so, what contributed to helping you learn that style?

✔ What career paths have you and your gender been encouraged to take in this and other organizations? Is this changing?

✔ Are both female and male styles of leadership equally valued or is one more valued in this organization? What gives you this impression? What style has been closer to acceptable management style in this organization? in other organizations? Is this changing?

✔ Are male leadership traits exhibited by both men and women equally in this organization? female leadership traits?

✔ What happens when men exhibit a more interactive style and women a more command and control style?

✔ What do you think the management style of choice will be in the future? Should a diversity of styles be valued? Should organizations expand their definition of what is effective leadership to include a combination of the best of both leadership styles?

4. Reconvene the entire group and have participants share highlights from their small group discussions.

Activity 3: Developmental Areas

1. Ask participants to circle the specific leadership traits they would like to develop and the kind of support they may need to develop those characteristics.

2. Have participants pair up with someone they feel can support them and discuss their developmental needs and how they might support one another.

3. After 20 minutes, reconvene the entire group and ask participants to share ways they plan to support their partners.

4. Encourage participants to become more well-rounded, effective leaders by using the best of both leadership styles.

VARIATIONS

■ Distribute reprints of the article "Ways Women Lead," available from *The Harvard Business Review*, reprint #90608, November–December, 1990.

■ Invite a senior management person to talk with your group about the kinds of leadership your organization needs in the future and how men and women can work together to be future leaders of the organization.

TYPICAL LEADERSHIP STYLES

Instructions: Check off (✔) the leadership characteristics that have been traditionally valued in organizations; star (★) the ones that will be most important for managing / leading organizations into the future. Also identify the advantages and disadvantages of using each particular trait in your organization.

Female Leadership Styles
(Transformational / Interactional Style)

Style	★/✔	Advantage	Disadvantage
Encourages participation (seeks input from others)			
Shares information & power (shares rationale, is candid)			
Enhances the self-worth of others (gives credit, praise, recognition)			
Energizes others (shows enthusiasm about work)			
Promotes teamwork			
Encourages creativity			
Balances concern for task with consideration of people and their needs			
Gets power from charisma, interpersonal skills, hard work			

TYPICAL LEADERSHIP STYLES, continued

Male Leadership Styles
(Transactional Style)

Style	★/✓	Advantage	Disadvantage
Leads by command and control			
Uses position power (power from organizational position & authority)			
Exchanges rewards for services or punishment for poor performance			
Task oriented			
Uses chain of command (quasi-military structure)			
Action oriented—is decisive and has conviction			
Thinks analytically and uses linear problem solving			

34 GENDER SCENARIOS

Participants use role plays to examine how to effectively handle work-place gender issues that concern them.

GOALS

To examine typical workplace situations that involve gender issues.

To learn to effectively handle workplace gender issues.

GROUP SIZE

10–20 participants (most effective with 20).

TIME

2–3 hours.

MATERIALS

Easels and easel paper; magic markers; masking tape; VCR; video camera; TV monitor.

☞ *The video equipment is optional. Activity 2 is more effective if the role plays are videotaped, but it is not essential.*

PROCESS

Activity 1: Typical Gender Scenarios

1. Briefly introduce the exercise with a chalktalk based on the following points:

   • More and more women today work outside the home—this organization, of course, has many female employees.

   • As you may have noticed, women and men often experience tension as they work together as colleagues.

   ○ Men often find themselves confused about how to treat women, unsure about simple issues such as whether they should let women get off the elevator first and also about more serious issues such as what constitutes sexual harassment.

○ Women are often resentful about how their male colleagues perceive and treat them—that they are seen as less competent or that their ideas are ignored or not given the same credibility as men's.

• In this session we want to openly explore some of these gender issues and find ways to effectively handle typical situations that may occur in the workplace.

2. Form mixed-gender groups of 4 participants and assign each group the following task:

➤ Discuss and identify some typical situations that occur between men and women in your workplace.

➤ Choose situations that you feel frustrated about or would like to explore how to handle more effectively.

➤ Record these situations on an easel sheet.

3. After about 20 minutes, call time, and reconvene the entire group.

4. Tape the lists on the walls and ask participants to take a marker and check off 4 they would most like to learn how to handle.

5. When they have finished, count the checks and, from those with the most checks, select the same number of scenarios as you have small groups.

Activity 2: Gender Role Play Preparation

☞ *Videotape this activity if the equipment is available to you and explain that you will erase the tape at the end of the exercise.*

1. Have participants rejoin their small groups and describe the role play process:

➤ I will assign each group a scenario to role play.

➤ Select members of your group to play specific roles.

➤ Prepare two role plays—one that demonstrates how not to respond to the situation and the other that demonstrates an effective way to handle the situation.

➤ You will have 15 minutes to prepare.

2. Have the subgroups move to separate spaces, assign a scenario to each, and tell them to develop their role plays.

©1995 Whole Person Press 210 W Michigan Duluth MN 55802   (800) 247-6789

Activity 3: Gender Role Plays

1. After about 15 minutes, call time and ask for a group to volunteer to present their role play of how not to handle a situation.

2. Stop the role play when it seems appropriate—when it is clear what not to do.

3. Play back the video (if you taped the role play), stopping at appropriate points to discuss the dynamics; get the entire group involved in a discussion by:

   a. asking the role players to talk about how they felt in their roles.

   b. asking the group to identify any gender dynamics that occurred in the scene.

4. Have the group present their role play on how to handle the situation in a more effective way.

5. Repeat *Step 3.*

   ☞ *If the participants have identified another, more effective way to handle the situation, ask the group to try role-playing using the new technique, and then discuss it.*

6. Thank the role players, move to the next group, and repeat *Steps 1–5* until each group has performed their role plays.

Activity 4: Workplace Gender Dynamics

1. Have participants rejoin their small groups to discuss the following questions:

   ☞ *Record these on an easel for all to see.*

   ✔ What major workplace gender dynamics occurred in the role plays?

   ✔ How can you respond differently at work now that you understand some of these dynamics?

   ✔ What will be difficult to tackle? easy?

   ✔ What will you start doing immediately in the workplace?

2. After about 20 minutes, reconvene the entire group and invite them to share what they learned.

VARIATIONS

■ If you want to shorten the time and already have some scenarios that you think are critical for the organization to examine, use those and eliminate *Steps 2–5* in Activity 1. (The main advantage to developing their own scenarios is that they tend to be more committed to the situations.) Some typical scenarios might include:

- In a meeting, a man uses off-color language and apologizes to the women present.

- A woman offers a suggestion in a meeting, but receives no verbal or nonverbal response to her suggestion. Several minutes later a man makes a similar suggestion and receives feedback from several other men about what a good idea he has.

- Prior to a staff meeting, a manager starts to tell a sexist joke. No women are present.

- In a meeting about moving the offices, a woman is asked to give the woman's point of view.

- A woman who manages the marketing team notices little condescending smirks and glances that the all-male executive board members give each other as she makes a proposal.

©1995 Whole Person Press 210 W Michigan Duluth MN 55802   (800) 247-6789

35 GENDER PERCEPTIONS

Designed for colleagues in the same organization, this exercise helps participants gain a better understanding of one another by identifying the type of gender bias men and women experience in the workplace.

GOALS

To identify the types of gender experiences that exist in our organization.

To reach a greater level of understanding among men and women in our organization.

GROUP SIZE

10–30 participants.

TIME

2 hours.

MATERIALS

Easels and easel paper; magic markers; masking tape.

PROCESS

Activity 1: Female and Male Experiences

1. Introduce the exercise by explaining that this activity tests how aware each gender is of the other gender experiences in the workplace.

2. Form same-gender groups, assign a facilitator to each group, and give them the following instructions:

   ➤ Discuss and develop a list of gender experiences you think the other group has had in this organization. For example, what experiences do women think men have in the organization.

   ➤ After you identify an experience, discuss what affect you think it has on the other group—what feelings it generates among the group's members.

   ➤ Your facilitator will record the experiences as you identify them. There does not have to be consensus for an item to be listed.

➤ Whatever anyone in the group thinks is the other's gender experience will be recorded.

3. Ask for questions about the task, move the groups to separate rooms, and have facilitators begin the task.

   ☞ *Facilitators should record experiences identified on an easel chart just as they are said—do not edit them. Participants should explore what they really think the other group experiences. Leave space on the right-hand side of the chart to list feelings/affects of each experience.*

Activity 2: Sharing Experiences

1. After about 45 minutes, reconvene the entire group.

2. Have the men sit in the center of the room in a circle facing each other as the women read their list for all to hear.

3. After the list of male gender experiences has been shared, allow the men to ask questions to clarify anything on the list.

4. Have the men respond to the accuracy of each item and add any key gender experiences the women missed.

   ☞ *Sometimes a group will identify an experience accurately, but will not understand the real impact that experience has. Make sure the group responds both to the accuracy of the experience and the accuracy of the impact on them. Responding allows for each gender group to discuss their experiences and be heard in a nondefensive atmosphere. Participants usually learn a great deal. If one group is really off target about the other group's experiences, you might want to ask what accounts for this lack of knowledge about the other gender's experiences.*

5. Repeat *Steps 2–4* with the women in the center and the men reading the list they created.

Activity 3: What Did We Learn?

1. Form mixed-gender groups of four (two men, two women) and discuss what they have learned from this session.

2. Reconvene the entire group and invite the small groups to share what they discussed.

©1995 Whole Person Press 210 W Michigan Duluth MN 55802   (800) 247-6789

36 GENDER MIRRORS

Participants share how they view the other gender, identify gender problems, and develop action plans to solve them—another exercise designed specifically for men and women who work together.

GOALS

To explore how women and men who work together perceive colleagues of the other gender.

To increase understanding between women and men colleagues.

To identify problems that exist between men and women who work together.

To develop some action plans to help men and women work together more effectively.

GROUP SIZE

Unlimited.

TIME

3–4 hours.

MATERIALS

Easels and easel paper; magic markers; masking tape; writing paper; pens and pencils.

PROCESS

Activity 1: Perceptions

1. Briefly introduce the exercise with the following chalktalk points:

   - In this session, the men will have an opportunity to explore how their female colleagues perceive them and the women will explore how the men they work with perceive them.

   - This information should help raise any gender issues or problems the organization may suffer from.

   - You will have time to identify any gender issues and examine how women and men can work together more effectively.

2. Form same-gender groups and assign them the following task:

  ➤ Create 3 lists of attributes: one illustrating how you perceive your gender in the organization, the second of how you see the other gender in the organization, and the third of what you think the other gender will say about you.

  ➤ The attributes can be both positive and negative, as long as they reflect what you truly believe.

     ☞ *Provide them with examples of attributes: self-assured, cocky, docile, calm, know-it-all, intelligent, diligent, underhanded, supportive, creative, enthusiastic, difficult, bossy, etc.*

  ➤ Remember, the focus is on the people in this organization, not men or women as a whole.

  ➤ In a moment, each group will go to a separate room and you will have 45 minutes to create your lists.

3. Have a facilitator take one of the groups to a separate room and begin the task.

     ☞ *Facilitators should record the lists created by each group. Have the assignment on an easel:*

     1.   How do we see ourselves in this organization?

     2.   How do we see the other gender group in this organization?

     3.   How do we think the other gender sees us?

Activity 2: Sharing Perceptions

1. After 45 minutes, reconvene the entire group and have the men share their list of how they perceive the organization's women (list #2).

   ☞ *As the lists are presented, allow only questions for clarification. Do not allow a debate about differences or let one group take issue with the other. The purpose of this phase is to present the data and seek understanding.*

2. After the men have finished, have the women share their lists of how they perceive themselves and what they thought the men would say (lists #1 and #3).

3. Have participants discuss the similarities and differences between the lists.

4. Repeat *Steps 1–3,* begin by asking the women to share how they perceive the organization's men.

©1995 Whole Person Press 210 W Michigan Duluth MN 55802   (800) 247-6789

Activity 3: Identifying Gender Problems

1. Hang all 6 lists on the wall and distribute paper and pencils to each participant.

2. Ask each person to review the lists individually and identify and record any problems they think exist between men and women in the organization.

3. Have the two gender groups meet again separately and consolidate their individual work into a group list.

   ☞ *Encourage them to discuss their individual items and to identify any problems not considered during the individual work.*

4. After about 30 minutes, reconvene the entire group and have each group present its list to the other, allowing only questions for clarification.

5. Ask for two volunteers from each group to work on consolidating the two lists while the others take a 10 minute break.

6. After the break, have the consolidation group report their work.

7. Ask the entire group to decide on the top 4 gender problems facing their organization, ones they want to work on in this group.

8. Form 4 mixed-gender groups, ask each to choose a different problem from the list of 4, and give them 20 minutes to work out a way to approach the problem.

9. Reconvene the entire group and ask each group to share its recommendations.

10. After each group has reported, invite participants to react to and discussion the recommendations.

11. Have the group decide on an action plan for each problem.

VARIATIONS

■ Instead of the 3 questions in Activity 1, *Step 3*, use the following questions if you want to deal more directly with conflict between the genders. What they would like to see the other gender stop doing? start doing? continue doing?

In Activity 2, first share #3, then #1, and last #2. Discuss and work toward mutual resolutions on items #1 and #2. This variation works well for a team or small group that has gender conflicts.

37 GENDER SUPPORT

Participants in the same organization identify ways they can support each other and identify behavior changes they need the other gender to make to help them be more successful and productive. Makes a great ending to a workshop.

GOALS

To identify ways men and women can support each other as well as ways they let each other down.

To discuss what women and men want from one another in the workplace.

To increase individual commitment to gender issues in a professional context.

GROUP SIZE

10–30 participants.

TIME

3 hours.

MATERIALS

Easels and easel paper; magic markers; masking tape.

PROCESS

Activity 1: Support

1. Briefly introduce the exercise by explaining that this session will help participants explore what women and men need from each other in order to be successful in the organization and that they will finish the session by making specific commitments to support one another in the future.

2. Form same-gender groups, assign each a separate workplace, and provide the following instructions:

   ➤ I have prepared 3 easel sheets for each group.

   ➤ The sheets for the women's group are titled:

1. On a day-to-day basis, men support women in these ways:

2. Men let women down in these ways:

3. Women could be more successful and productive if men would:

➤ The sheets for the men's group are titled:

1. On a day-to-day basis, women support men in these ways:

2. Women let men down in these ways:

3. Men could be more successful and productive if women would:

➤ On the left side of each page, in a single column list words and phrases to complete the starter sentence.

➤ You have 30 minutes. Begin.

Activity 2: Reporting Results

1. After 30 minutes, reconvene the entire group and have the women read their list of how the men support them on a daily basis (list #1).

   ☞ *Allow any questions of clarification from the men.*

2. Have the men read their list of how the women support them on a daily basis (list #1).

   ☞ *Allow any questions of clarification from the women.*

3. Beginning with the men, repeat *Steps 1* and *2* using their lists of how the other gender lets them down (list #2).

4. Beginning with the women, repeat *Steps 1* and *2* using their lists of how each gender wants the other to support them (list #3).

5. Invite participants to share any observations or insights about what they think the information they generated means.

Activity 3: Negotiating Wants and Making Commitments

1. Inform participants that they will now spend time examining what each group wants from the other, identifying priorities and making commitments to help one another.

2. On each group's list of what would make them more successful, draw vertical lines dividing the right hand side of the page into 3 columns. Title the columns:

   • Seriousness

   • Frequency of occurrence

- Able to be accomplished

3. Create a grid by drawing horizontal lines the width of the paper under each word or phrase on the list.

   ☞ *You should now have a chart with a box across from each item and under each title.*

4. Have participants discuss each item on the list of what men want from women and place a high (H), medium (M), or low (L) priority level in each box under the appropriate category.

   ☞ *The goal is to prioritize the issues and choose two or three items to examine further.*

5. Repeat *Steps 4* using the list of what the women want from the men.

6. Have participants rejoin their same-gender groups and assign the following task:

   ➤ Discuss and work with the two or three priority items the other gender would like you to help them with.

   ➤ Examine each item by listing what you would gain or lose by making a commitment to accomplish that item.

7. After 30 minutes, reconvene the entire group and have each gender group report their discussions to the other.

8. Have the gender groups negotiate terms to which they agree to help one another with each issue.

   ☞ *Make sure the agreements are realistic and that each group truly commits itself to living up to the agreement.*

9. End with an appropriate way of celebrating their commitments, such as proposing a toast to one another.

READING LIST

Allen, Robert L. and Herb Boyd, editors. *Brotherman: An Anthology of Writings by and about Black Men*. New York: Ballantine, 1993.

Baraff, Alvin. *Men Talk*. New York: Dutton, 1991.

Connell, R.W. *Gender and Power*. Stanford, Calif.: Stanford University Press, 1987.

Dinnerstein, Dorothy. *The Mermaid and the Minotaur: Sexual Arrangements and Human Malaise*. New York: Harper & Row, 1976.

Eisler, Riane. *The Chalice and the Blade*. San Francisco: HarperCollins, 1988.

Elgin, Suzette Haden. *Genderspeak*. New York: John Wiley & Sons, 1993.

Farrell, Warren. *The Liberated Man*. New York: Random House, 1975.

Fasteau, Marc. *The Male Machine*. New York: Dell Publishing Company, 1975.

French, Marilyn. *Beyond Power: On Women, Men and Morals*. New York: Summit Books, 1985.

Glass, Lillian. *He Says, She Says*. New York: Putnam, 1992.

Gray, John. *Men are From Mars, Women are From Venus*. New York: HarperCollins, 1992.

Hagan, Kay Leigh. *Women Respond to the Men's Movement*. San Francisco: HarperCollins, 1992.

Haki, Madhubuti. *Black Men: Obsolete, Single, Dangerous?* Chicago: Third World Press, 1991.

Hearn, Jeff. *The Gender of Oppression*. New York: St. Martin's Press, 1987.

Heilbrun, Carolyn G. *Toward a Recognition of Androgyny*. New York: W.W. Norton, 1973.

Helgesen, Sally. *The Female Advantage: Women's Way of Leadership*. New York: Doubleday, 1990.

Kanter, Rosabeth Moss. *Men and Women of the Corporation*. New York: Basic Books, 1977.

Keen, Sam. *Fire in the Belly*. New York: Bantam Books, 1992.

©1995 Whole Person Press 210 W Michigan Duluth MN 55802   (800) 247-6789

Kimmel, Michael, ed. *Changing Men: New Directions in Research on Men and Masculinity.* Newbury Park, Calif.: Sage Publications, 1987.

——. and Michael Messner. *Men's Lives.* New York: Macmillan, 1992.

——. *Manhood: The American Quest.* New York: HarperCollins, 1994.

Lakoff, R. *Talking Power: The Politics of Language in our Lives.* New York: Basic Books, 1990.

Lorber, Judith. *Paradoxes of Gender.* New York: Yale University Press, 1994.

Levine, Judith. *My Enemy, My Love: Women, Men and the Dilemmas of Gender.* New York: Doubleday, 1993.

Miedzian, Myriam. *Boys Will Be Boys: Breaking the Link Between Masculinity and Violence.* New York: Doubleday, 1991.

Pleck, Joseph. *The Myth of Masculinity.* Cambridge, Mass.: M.I.T. Press, 1981.

Pleck, Joseph and Jack Sawyer, ed. *Men and Masculinity.* Englewood Cliffs, N.J.: Prentice-Hall, 1974.

Sargent, Alice. *The Androgynous Manager.* New York: American Management Association, 1983.

Sargent, Alice. *Beyond Sex Roles.* New York: West Publishing Company, 1985.

Segal, Lynne. *Slow Motion: Changing Masculinity*, Changing Men. New Brunswick, N.J.: Rutgers Unaiversity, 1990.

Snodgrass, Jon, ed. *For Men Against Sexism: A Book of Readings.* Albion, Calif.: Times Change Press, 1977.

Spender, Dale. *Men's Studies Modified: The Impact of Feminism on the Academic Disciplines.* New York: Pergamon Press, Athene Series, 1987.

——. *Man Made Language.* London: Routledge and Kegan Paul, 1980.

Steinem, Gloria. *Revolution From Within.* Boston: Little, Brown, 1992.

Stoltenberg, John. *Refusing to be a Man.* New York: Penguin, 1990.

Tannen, Deborah. *Talking from 9 to 5.* New York: William Morrow, 1994.

——. *You Just Don't Understand.* New York: William Morrow, 1990.

Tingley, Judith. *Genderflex.* New York: American Management Association, 1994.

©1995 Whole Person Press 210 W Michigan Duluth MN 55802   (800) 247-6789

TRAINER'S NOTES

How to Use This Book Most Effectively

THE CONCEPT OF EXPERIENTIAL LEARNING

As you will notice with just a cursory glance through this volume, these educational experiences actively involve participants in the learning process. Why? Because when you draw on the resources of the group in your presentations, you empower people.

Every session in this book balances didactic information and group participation. Experiential training concentrates on developing awareness and understanding plus building skills that can be used at home and on the job. This model helps participants become involved and therefore makes it more likely they will assume responsibility for their own learning.

Each exercise is designed to create opportunities for participants to interact with the concepts and each other in meaningful ways. The lecture method is replaced with succinct chalktalks and facilitative questions that guide people to discover their own answers. The authority of the trainer is transformed into the authority of the individual's inner wisdom.

THE TRAINER'S CHALLENGE

For many teachers, giving up the authority implicit in the typical lecture format is a risky proposition. Trainers are often afraid that they won't be perceived as an expert, so they are tempted to lecture, entertain and keep the focus on themselves. Yet, if your goal is truly to help people change, information is not enough. Praise from your audience is not enough. What really counts are the discoveries participants make about their own patterns and the choices they make to manage their lives more effectively.

Remember, as a trainer, you are not presenting a paper at a conference. You are engaging an audience in an educational process. Your task is to appeal to people with different learning styles, using a wide variety of strategies to get them involved. In whole person learning, the questions are as important as the content.

THE TEACHING STRATEGIES

These exercises help you involve people in the process of reflecting, prioritizing, sorting, and planning for change by using the following strategies.

1. **Activating participants' internal wisdom**: This is best accomplished by asking questions that help people come up with answers that are right for them, rather than by giving them your "right answers."

©1995 Whole Person Press 210 W Michigan Duluth MN 55802   (800) 247-6789

2. **Helping people make choices**: These exercises assist people to sort out their own values and priorities, helping them to explore their beliefs and assumptions and encouraging them to alter their lives in ways that they choose, based on their own sense of rhythm and timing.

3. **Activating the group's resources**: These exercises take the dynamic of the group seriously. The first five minutes are the key! They help you get people involved with each other right off the bat, and let you use and work with the energy of the group—the laughter, the group norms, the embarrassment, the competition.

4. **Fostering interpersonal support**: With these exercises you capitalize on the rich variety of experiences and insights among your participants. And you capitalize on the power of their support for each other. Interaction builds trust, helps people consider new options, and offers support for change. For many people this chance to compare notes with others is the most powerful part of the session.

THE RHYTHM OF EACH SESSION

To accomplish these teaching objectives each exercise is designed to include a rhythmic sequence of activities with enough change of pace to keep the group's involvement and energy high. Most exercises include:

A warm-up—An introductory activity that gets people involved with each other around the subject in an energetic and playful manner.

A chalktalk—A brief introduction to the session's main concepts.

Personal reflection—Questions to help each participant test the concepts against their own life experiences in order to determine which ideas make sense to them.

Inductive summary—A pooling of the group's observations and insights.

Planning/commitment—The bottom line in training. Everyone should leave the session with at least one clear idea about what they will do next.

THE FORMAT

The format of this book is designed for easy use. Every exercise is described completely, including goals, group size, time, materials needed, step-by-step process instructions, and variations. The format employs the following symbols to help indicate specific items:

☞ *Special instructions for the trainer are set in italics and preceded by a pointing hand.*

✔ Questions to ask participants are preceded by a check.

➤ Instructions for group activities are indicated by an arrow.

● Chalktalk (mini-lecture) notes and sentence-completion fragments are preceded by a bullet.

Time: The time frame provided at the beginning of each exercise and times given for various activities within the process are only guidelines—suggestions to help you organize and schedule a successful workshop. Feel free to adapt the times as you feel necessary.

Worksheets: Many of the exercises include worksheets for participants to complete. The worksheets can be found immediately following the exercises in which they are to be used. Make certain you photocopy enough worksheets for all your participants prior to conducting an exercise. (8 1/2" x 11" photocopy masters for this book are also available from Whole Person Associates.)

Chalktalks: Most of the exercises include chalktalk notes—bulleted lists of information that help introduce an exercise or provide vital information on its topic. These notes provide a framework to help you develop a complete mini-lecture of your own.

TIPS FOR USING THESE EXERCISES MOST EFFECTIVELY

1. **Tailor your process to the group**: Read the objectives for each exercise and carefully choose those you will use. Remember, these exercises are more than fun and games. Each one has a clear purpose.

   Decide what is appropriate based on the setting, the time available, the purpose and the participants' style and comfort level. Exercises should be specifically selected for a particular organization and should be tailored to that organization's style and culture. What will work well in one situation may not work as effectively in another. Feel free to adapt exercises as you deem necessary.

2. **Pay attention to the timing**: In your planning, anticipate the needs and rhythm of the group. At the first session you'll need more time for setting the ground rules and getting acquainted. In later sessions, as people get to know each other better you'll need to allocate more time for the discussion segments.

   Every group goes through predictable (and unpredictable!) cycles. Anticipate peak times and down times during the day and plan for changing the pace as needed to restore energy and enthusiasm.

©1995 Whole Person Press 210 W Michigan Duluth MN 55802   (800) 247-6789

3. **Prepare yourself thoroughly for each session**: Good teaching is built on examples and anecdotes. In order to make the material come alive for you and for others, you will need to carefully work through each session and personalize each segment with your own examples and stories. You can do this in a number of ways:

- Read the detailed exercise outline thoroughly. Be sure you understand the basic concepts and processes for the session. Answer all worksheet questions for yourself. This will help you anticipate difficulties and will provide you with lively personal examples.

- Reread the chalktalk notes one point at a time. Translate the ideas into your own words. Personalize each concept with carefully chosen examples that you think will fit the group's needs.

- Add diagrams, cartoons, newspaper articles—whatever relevant information you come across during your preparation.

- Relax. Take a few minutes by yourself before you begin each session so that you are centered and focused.

4. **Make the environment work for you**: The room makes a very important contribution to the atmosphere. The best location has soft lighting, comfortable chairs, is neither too big nor too small, and has privacy to prevent interruptions that would distract the group. If you must meet in a room that's too large, keep the group together. Don't let people spread out all over—distance breeds isolation.

Banked auditoriums with fixed seats are workable, but not recommended. The inflexibility of the seating makes movement exercises and small group gatherings more difficult.

Encourage participants to sit in a circle. This creates the most successful setting since it provides an ideal forum for verbal and nonverbal communication and offers an atmosphere of inclusion.

You will want to have a chalkboard or sheets of newsprint (or both!) available for your use at all times.

Don't expect anyone else to set up the room for you. Get there early and if necessary, set it up yourself.

5. **Establish a supportive atmosphere**: Participants in your sessions must feel safe enough to examine their attitudes and beliefs and to change some of them. A trainer open to listening to what all participants say creates an atmosphere of security.

Always restate a participant's comment or question before you respond. Summarizing what you heard affirms the person and shows your audience that you are listening and taking them seriously.

Begin the workshop with a discussion of guidelines for the session. This helps alleviate anxiety and sets a positive tone. Suggestions include: attend regularly and be on time, listen to each other carefully, and respect confidentiality.

6. **Carefully plan the small group discussions**: For most discussions, groups of four to six are optimal. Timing will be a problem if some groups have three people and others have eight. So try to keep groups the same size as indicated in the instructions.

In many exercises your leader notes tell you how to divide the participants into small groups. In others the "how to" is left up to you.

If some people don't participate (or even leave the room during group sharing time) don't panic. Don't drop the group experience because a few people feel uncomfortable. For many people the small group discussions are the most valuable part of the session.

7. **Grow from this experience yourself**: Try to learn the most you can from every event. Don't be afraid to share yourself. You are a leader/participant! Don't be discouraged if each session does not go exactly as you had expected. Turn disasters into opportunities. When something does not go well, laugh! When all else fails, start asking questions.

Plan to have fun! The processes in these exercises are designed so that you have a chance to listen as well as talk. The whole experience does not depend on you. Open your eyes and your ears, you'll learn something too!

©1995 Whole Person Press 210 W Michigan Duluth MN 55802   (800) 247-6789

Whole Person Associates Resources

All printed, audio, and video resources developed by Whole Person Associates are designed to address the whole person—physical, emotional, mental, spiritual, and social. On the next pages, trainers will find a wide array of resources that offer ready-to-use ideas and concepts they can add to their programs.

GROUP PROCESS RESOURCES

All of the exercises in these group process resources encourage interaction between the leader and participants, as well as among the participants. Each exercise includes everything needed to present a meaningful program.

WORKING WITH WOMEN'S GROUPS
Volumes 1 & 2
Louise Yolton Eberhardt

The two volumes of **Working with Women's Groups** have been completely revised and updated. **Volume 1** explores consciousness raising, self-discovery, and assertiveness training. **Volume 2** looks at sexuality issues, women of color, and leadership skills training.

❑ **Working with Women's Groups**
Volumes 1 & 2 / $24.95 per volume

WORKING WITH MEN'S GROUPS
Roger Karsk and Bill Thomas

Working with Men's Groups has been updated to reflect the reality of men's lives in the 1990s. Each exercise follows a structured pattern to help trainers develop either one-time workshops or ongoing groups that explore men's issues in four key areas: self-discovery, consciousness raising, intimacy, and parenting.

❑ **Working with Men's Groups / $24.95**

WORKSHEET MASTERS
Complete packages of (8 1/2" x 11") photocopy masters are available for **Working with Women's Groups** and **Working with Men's Groups**. Use the masters to conveniently duplicate handouts for each participant.

❑ **Worksheet Masters / $9.95 per volume**

To order, call toll free   (800) 247-6789

WORKING WITH GROUPS IN THE WORKPLACE

This new collection addresses the special needs and concerns of trainers in the workplace. As the work force changes, EAP counselors, education departments, and management are being called on to guide and support their employees who face the challenges of a more diverse workplace.

BRIDGING THE GENDER GAP
Louise Yolton Eberhardt

Bridging the Gender Gap contains a wealth of exercises for the trainer to use with men and women who work as colleagues. These activities will also be useful in gender role awareness groups, diversity training, couples workshops, college classes, and youth seminars.

❏ **Bridging the Gender Gap / $24.95**

CONFRONTING SEXUAL HARASSMENT
Louise Yolton Eberhardt

Confronting Sexual Harassment presents exercises that trainers can safely use with groups to constructively explore the issues of sexual harassment, look at the underlying causes, understand the law, motivate men to become allies, and empower women to speak up.

❏ **Confronting Sexual Harassment / $24.95**

CELEBRATING DIVERSITY
Cheryl Hetherington

Celebrating Diversity helps people confront and question the beliefs, prejudices, and fears that can separate them from others. Carefully written exercises help trainers present these sensitive issues in the workplace as well as in educational settings.

❏ **Celebrating Diversity / $24.95**

WORKSHEET MASTERS
Complete packages of (8 1/2" x 11") photocopy masters are available for all books in the **Working with Groups in the Workplace** series.

❏ **Worksheet Masters / $9.95 per volume**

To order, call toll free   (800) 247-6789

STRESS AND WELLNESS ANNOTATED GUIDES

From worksite health promotion to life-style research to family stress, these authoritative reviews of classic and contemporary information sources will help you locate the resources you need for planning workshops, classes, program proposals, or presentations on stress and wellness.

STRESS RESOURCES

An annotated guide to essential books, periodicals, A-V materials and teaching tools about stress for trainers, consultants, counselors, educators and health professionals

Selected and reviewed by Jim Polidora, Ph.D.

Jim Polidora reviews the best current and classic, popular and scientific literature in every area of stress management. Over 500 annotations are arranged topically for easy reference.

Each of the fifteen chapters includes reviews of books and audiovisual resources. Special sections feature textbooks, catalogs, journals, newsletters, and stress-related organizations.

❏ **Stress Resources / $34.95**

WELLNESS RESOURCES

An annotated guide to essential books, periodicals, A-V materials and teaching tools about wellness for trainers, consultants, counselors, educators and health professionals

Selected and reviewed by Jim Polidora, Ph.D.

This first comprehensive guide to wellness resources is packed with descriptions of over 500 of the best current and classic books, audiotapes, videotapes, journals, newsletters, and catalogs.

The fifteen chapters of reading and viewing suggestions in **Wellness Resources** make workshop or program planning a breeze.

❏ **Wellness Resources / $34.95**

To order, call toll free   (800) 247-6789

STRUCTURED EXERCISES IN STRESS MANAGEMENT

Nancy Loving Tubesing, EdD, and Donald A. Tubesing, PhD, Editors

Each book in this four-volume series contains 36 ready-to-use teaching modules that involve the participant—as a whole person—in learning how to manage stress more effectively.

Each volume brims with practical ideas that mix and match allowing trainers to develop new programs for varied settings, audiences, and time frames. Each volume contains **Icebreakers, Stress Assessments, Management Strategies, Skill Builders, Action Planners, Closing Processes,** and **Group Energizers**.

❏ **Stress 8 1/2" x 11" Loose-Leaf Edition—Volume 1-4 / $54.95 each**
❏ **Stress 6" x 9" Softcover Edition—Volume 1-4 / $29.95 each**

STRUCTURED EXERCISES IN WELLNESS PROMOTION

Nancy Loving Tubesing, EdD, and Donald A. Tubesing, PhD, Editors

Each of the four volumes in this innovative series includes 36 experiential learning activities that focus on whole person health—body, mind, spirit, emotions, relationships, and life-style.

Icebreakers, Wellness Explorations, Self-Care Strategies, Action Planners, Closings, and **Group Energizers** are all ready-to-go—including reproducible worksheets, scripts, and chalktalk outlines—for the busy professional who wants to develop unique wellness programs without spending hours in preparation.

❏ **Wellness 8 1/2" x 11" Loose-Leaf Edition—Volume 1-4 / $54.95 each**
❏ **Wellness 6" x 9" Softcover Edition—Volume 1-4 / $29.95 each**

WORKSHEET MASTERS

Complete packages of (8 1/2" x 11") photocopy masters are available for all **Structured Exercises in Stress Management** and **Structured Exercises in Wellness Promotion**. Use the masters to conveniently duplicate handouts for each participant.

❏ **Worksheet Masters / $9.95 per volume**

To order, call toll free   (800) 247-6789

RELAXATION AUDIOTAPES

Perhaps you're an old hand at relaxation, looking for new ideas. Or maybe you're a beginner, just testing the waters. Whatever your relaxation needs, Whole Person audiotapes provide a whole family of options for reducing physical and mental stress.

Techniques range from simple breathing and stretching exercises to classic autogenic and progressive relaxation sequences, guided meditations, and whimsical daydreams. All are carefully crafted to promote whole person relaxation—body, mind, and spirit.

If you're looking for an extended relaxation experience (20 minutes or more), try a tape from the Sensational Relaxation, Guided Imagery, or Wilderness Daydreams groups. For quick R&R breaks (5–10 minutes), try a Stress Breaks, Daydreams or Mini-Meditations collections. All of our tapes feature male and female narrators.

Audiotapes are available for $11.95 each.
Call for generous quantity discounts.

SENSATIONAL RELAXATION—$11.95 each

When stress piles up, it becomes a heavy load both physically and emotionally. These full-length relaxation experiences will teach you techniques that can be used whenever you feel that stress is getting out of control. Choose one you like and repeat it daily until it becomes second nature, then recall that technique whenever you need it or try a new one every day.

- ❑ **Countdown to Relaxation /** Countdown 19:00, Staircase 19:00
- ❑ **Daybreak / Sundown /** Daybreak 22:00, Sundown 22:00
- ❑ **Take a Deep Breath /** Breathing for Relaxation 17:00, Magic Ball 17:00
- ❑ **Relax . . . Let Go . . . Relax /** Revitalization 27:00, Relaxation 28:00
- ❑ **StressRelease /** Quick Tension Relievers 22:00,Progressive Relaxation 20:00
- ❑ **Warm and Heavy /** Warm 24:00, Heavy 23:00

STRESS BREAKS—$11.95 each

Do you need a short energy booster or a quick stress reliever? If you don't know what type of relaxation you like, or if you are new to guided relaxation techniques, try one of our Stress Breaks for a quick refocusing or change of pace any time of the day.

- ❑ **BreakTime /** Solar Power 8:00, Belly Breathing 9:00, Fortune Cookie 9:00, Mother Earth 11:00, Big Yawn 5:00, Affirmation 11:00
- ❑ **Natural Tranquilizers /** Clear the Deck 10:00, Body Scan 10:00, 99 Countdown 10:00, Calm Down 9:00, Soothing Colors 11:00, Breathe Ten 9:00

To order, call toll free   (800) 247-6789

DAYDREAMS—$11.95 each

Escape from the stress around you with guided tours to beautiful places. The quick escapes in our Daydreams tapes will lead your imagination away from your everyday cares so you can resume your tasks relaxed and comforted.

- ❑ **Daydreams 1: Getaways /** Cabin Retreat 11:00, Night Sky 10:00, Hot Spring 7:00, Mountain View 8:00, Superior Sail 8:00
- ❑ **Daydreams 2: Peaceful Places /** Ocean Tides 11:00, City Park 10:00, Hammock 8:00, Meadow 11:00
- ❑ **Daydreams 3: Relaxing Retreats /** Melting Candle 5:00, Tropical Paradise 10:00, Sanctuary 7:00, Floating Clouds 5:00, Seasons 9:00, Beach Tides 9:00

GUIDED MEDITATION—$11.95 each

Take a step beyond relaxation. The imagery in our full-length meditations will help you discover your strengths, find healing, make positive life changes, and recognize your inner wisdom.

- ❑ **Inner Healing /** Inner Healing 20:00, Peace with Pain 20:00
- ❑ **Personal Empowering /** My Gifts 22:00, Hidden Strengths 21:00
- ❑ **Healthy Balancing /** Inner Harmony 20:00, Regaining Equilibrium 20:00
- ❑ **Spiritual Centering /** Spiritual Centering 20:00 (male and female narration)

WILDERNESS DAYDREAMS—$11.95 each

Discover the healing power of nature with the four tapes in our Wilderness Daydreams series. The eight special journeys will transport you from your harried, stressful surroundings to the peaceful serenity of words and water.

- ❑ **Canoe / Rain /** Canoe 19:00, Rain 22:00
- ❑ **Island / Spring /** Island 19:00, Spring 19:00
- ❑ **Campfire / Stream /** Campfire 17:00, Stream 19:00
- ❑ **Sailboat / Pond /** Sailboat 25:00, Pond 25:00

MINI-MEDITATIONS—$11.95 each

These brief guided visualizations begin by focusing your breathing and uncluttering your mind, so that you can concentrate on a sequence of sensory images that promote relaxation, centering, healing, growth, and spiritual awareness.

- ❑ **Healing Visions /** Rocking Chair 5:00, Pine Forest 8:00, Long Lost Confidant 10:00, Caterpillar to Butterfly 7:00, Superpowers 9:00, Tornado 8:00
- ❑ **Refreshing Journeys /** 1 to 10 10:00, Thoughts Library 11:00, Visualizing Change 6:00, Magic Carpet 9:00, Pond of Love 9:00, Cruise 9:00

MUSIC ONLY—$11.95 each

No relaxation program would be complete without relaxing melodies that can be played as background to a prepared script or that can be enjoyed as you practice a technique you have already learned. Steven Eckels composed his melodies specifically for relaxation. These "musical prayers for healing" will calm your body, mind, and spirit.

- ❑ **Tranquility /** Awakening 20:00, Repose 20:00
- ❑ **Harmony /** Waves of Light 30:00, Rising Mist 10:00, Frankincense 10:00, Angelica 10:00
- ❑ **Serenity /** Radiance 20:00, Quiessence 10:00, Evanesence 10:00

To order, call toll free (800) 247-6789

RELAXATION RESOURCES

Many trainers and workshop leaders have discovered the benefits of relaxation and visualization in healing the body, mind, and spirit.

30 SCRIPTS FOR RELAXATION, IMAGERY, AND INNER HEALING
Julie Lusk

The relaxation scripts, creative visualizations and guided meditations in these volumes were created by experts in the field of guided imagery. Julie Lusk collected their best and most effective scripts to help novices get started and experienced leaders expand their repertoire. Both volumes include information on how to use the scripts, suggestions for tailoring them to specific needs and audiences, and information on how to successfully incorporate guided imagery into existing programs.

❑ **30 Scripts**
   Volume 1 & 2 / $19.95 each

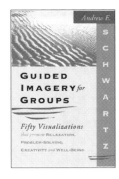

GUIDED IMAGERY FOR GROUPS
Andrew Schwartz

Ideal for courses, workshops, team building, and personal stress management, this comprehensive resource includes scripts for 50 thematic visualizations that promote calming, centering, creativity, congruence, clarity, coping, and connectedness. Detailed instructions for using relaxation techniques and guided images in group settings allow educators at all levels, in any setting, to help people tap into the healing and creative powers of imagery.

❑ **Guided Imagery for Groups / $24.95**

INQUIRE WITHIN
Andrew Schwartz

Use visualization to help people make positive changes in their life. The 24 visualization experiences in **Inquire Within** will help participants enhance their creativity, heal inner pain, learn to relax, and deal with conflict. Each visualization includes questions at the end of the process that encourage deeper reflection and a better understanding of the exercise and the response it evokes.

❑ **Inquire Within / $19.95**

To order, call toll free   (800) 247-6789

PLAYFUL ACTIVITIES FOR POWERFUL PRESENTATIONS
Bruce Williamson

Spice up presentations with healthy laughter. The 40 creative energizers in *Playful Activities for Powerful Presentations* will enhance learning, stimulate communication, promote teamwork, and reduce resistance to group interaction.

This potent but light-hearted resource will make presentations on any topic more powerful and productive.

❑ Playful Activities for Powerful Presentations $19.95

WORKING WITH GROUPS FROM DYSFUNCTIONAL FAMILIES
Cheryl Hetherington

Even the healthiest family can be dysfunctional at times, making everyone vulnerable to the pain of difficult family relationships.

This collection of 29 proven group activities is designed to heal the pain that results from living in a dysfunctional family. With these exercises leaders can promote healing, build self-esteem, encourage sharing, and help participants acknowledge their feelings.

❑ Working with Groups from Dysfunctional Families / $24.95

WORKSHEET MASTERS
A complete package of (8 1/2" x 11") photocopy masters is available for **Working with Groups from Dysfunctional Families**. Use the masters to conveniently duplicate handouts for each participant.

❑ Worksheet Masters / $9.95 per volume

To order, call toll free   (800) 247-6789

VIDEO RESOURCES

These video-based workshops use the power of professionally produced videotapes as a starting point. Then they build on the experience with printed guides chock-full of suggestions, group processes, and personal growth exercises that build sessions participants will remember!

MAKING HEALTHY CHOICES

Making Healthy Choices, a complete six-session, video-based course on healthy living, encourages people to begin making the choices, large and small, that promote wellness in all areas of their lives. Save $95.00 by purchasing the complete set or select individual sessions.

- ❑ **MAKING HEALTHY CHOICES SET / $474.00**
- ❑ **Healthy Lifestyle / $95.00**
- ❑ **Healthy Eating / $95.00**
- ❑ **Healthy Exercise / $95.00**
- ❑ **Healthy Stress / $95.00**
- ❑ **Healthy Relationships / $95.00**
- ❑ **Healthy Change / $95.00**

MANAGING JOB STRESS

Managing Job Stress, a comprehensive six-session stress management course, takes aim at a universal problem: work-related stress. Each session emphasizes positive responses to the challenges of on-the-job stress. Save $95.00 by purchasing the entire set or select individual sessions.

- ❑ **MANAGING JOB STRESS SET / $474.00**
- ❑ **Handling Workplace Pressure / $95.00**
- ❑ **Clarifying Roles and Expectations / $95.00**
- ❑ **Controlling the Workload / $95.00**
- ❑ **Managing People Pressures / $95.00**
- ❑ **Surviving the Changing Workplace / $95.00**
- ❑ **Balancing Work and Home / $95.00**

MANAGE IT!

Manage It! is an innovative six-part video-based series that helps participants develop management skills for handling stress. Participants learn new coping skills and practice a relaxation technique for immediate on-the-spot stress relief. Save $95.00 by purchasing the entire set or select individual sessions.

- ❑ **MANAGE IT! SET / $474.00**
- ❑ **Stress Traps / $95.00**
- ❑ **Stress Overload / $95.00**
- ❑ **Interpersonal Conflict / $95.00**
- ❑ **Addictive Patterns / $95.00**
- ❑ **Job Stress / $95.00**
- ❑ **Survival Skills / $95.00**

To order, call toll free   (800) 247-6789

WORKSHOPS-IN-A-BOOK

Workshops-in-a-book are developed to be used as a classroom text, discussion guide, and participant workbook; a professional resource for both novice and experienced trainers; a personal journey for individuals; all in an easy-to-understand, user-friendly format.

KICKING YOUR STRESS HABITS:
A Do-it-yourself Guide for Coping with Stress
Donald A. Tubesing, PhD

Over a quarter of a million people have found ways to deal with their everyday stress by using **Kicking Your Stress Habits**. This workshop-in-a-book actively involves the reader in assessing stressful patterns and developing more effective coping strategies with helpful "Stop and Reflect" sections in each chapter.

The 10-step planning process and 20 skills for managing stress make **Kicking Your Stress Habits** an ideal text for stress management classes in many different settings, from hospitals to universities.

❏ **Kicking Your Stress Habits / $14.95**

SEEKING YOUR HEALTHY BALANCE:
A Do-it-yourself Guide to Whole Person Well-being
Donald A. Tubesing, PhD and Nancy Loving Tubesing, EdD

Where can people find the time and energy to "do it all" without sacrificing health and well-being? **Seeking Your Healthy Balance** helps readers discover how to develop a more balanced life-style by learning effective ways to juggle work, self, and others; by clarifying self-care options; and by discovering and setting their own personal priorities.

Seeking Your Healthy Balance asks the questions that help readers find their own answers.

❏ **Seeking Your Healthy Balance / $14.95**

To order, call toll free   (800) 247-6789

WELLNESS ACTIVITIES FOR YOUTH
Volumes 1 & 2
Sandy Queen

Each volume of **Wellness Activities for Youth** provides 36 complete classroom activities that help leaders teach children and teenagers about wellness with a whole person approach and an emphasis on FUN.

The concepts include:

- values
- stress and coping
- self-esteem
- personal well-being
- social wellness

❏ **Wellness Activities for Youth Volume 1 & 2 / $19.95 each**

WORKSHEET MASTERS
Complete packages of (8 1/2" x 11") photocopy masters are available for each volume of **Wellness Activities for Youth**. Use the masters to conveniently duplicate handouts for each participant.

❏ **Worksheet Masters / $9.95 per volume**

WHAT DO YOU DO WITH A CHILD LIKE THIS?
L. Tobin

What Do You Do With A Child Like This? takes readers on a journey inside the world of troubled children, inviting empathy, then presenting a variety of proven techniques for helping these children to make the behavior changes that will bring them happier lives. This unique book, filled with innovative and practical tools for teachers, psychologists, and parents has been praised by educators for its sensitivity to the pain of troubled kids.

❏ **What Do You Do With A Child Like This? / $14.95**

To order, call toll free   (800) 247-6789

About Whole Person Associates

At Whole Person Associates, we're 100% committed to providing stress and wellness materials that involve participants and provide a "whole person" focus—body, mind, spirit, and relationships.

That's our mission and it's very important to us—but it doesn't tell the whole story. Behind the products in our catalog is a company full of people—and *that's* what really makes us who we are.

ABOUT THE OWNERS
Whole Person Associates was created by the vision of two people: Donald A. Tubesing, PhD, and Nancy Loving Tubesing, EdD. Since way back in 1970, Don and Nancy have been active in the stress management/wellness promotion movement—consulting, leading seminars, writing, and publishing. Most of our early products were the result of their creativity and expertise.

Living proof that you can "stay evergreen," Don and Nancy remain the driving force behind the company and are still very active in developing new products that touch people's lives.

ABOUT THE COMPANY
Whole Person Associates was "born" in Duluth, Minnesota, and we remain committed to our lovely city on the shore of Lake Superior. All of our operations are here, which makes communication between departments much easier! We've grown since our beginnings, but at a steady pace—we're interested in sustainable growth that allows us to keep our down-to-earth orientation.

We put the same high quality into every product we offer, translating the best of current research into practical, accessible, easy-to-use materials. In this way we can create the best possible resources to help our customers teach about stress management and wellness promotion.

We also strive to treat our customers as we would like to be treated. If we fall short of our goals in any way, please let us know.

ABOUT OUR EMPLOYEES
Speaking of down-to-earth, that's a requirement for each and every one of our employees. We're all product consultants, which means that anyone who answers the phone can probably answer your questions (if they can't, they'll find someone who can.)

We focus on helping you find the products that fit your needs. And we've found that the best way to accomplish that is by hiring friendly and resourceful people.

ABOUT OUR ASSOCIATES

Who are the "associates" in Whole Person Associates? They're the trainers, authors, musicians, and others who have developed much of the material you see on these pages. We're always on the lookout for high-quality products that reflect our "whole person" philosophy and fill a need for our customers.

Most of our products were developed by experts who are at the top of their fields, and we're very proud to be associated with them.

ABOUT OUR CUSTOMERS

Finally, we wouldn't have a reason to exist without you, our customers. We've met some of you, and we've talked to many more of you on the phone. We are always aware that without you, there would be no Whole Person Associates.

That's why we'd love to hear from you! Let us know what you think of our products—how you use them in your work, what additional products you'd like to see, and what shortcomings you've noted. Write us or call on our toll-free line. We look forward to hearing from you!